THIRD EDITION

RESUMES FOR HIGH SCHOOL GRADUATES

With Sample Cover Letters

The Editors of McGraw-Hill

McGraw·Hill

New York   Chicago   San Francisco   Lisbon   London   Madrid   Mexico City
Milan   New Delhi   San Juan   Seoul   Singapore   Sydney   Toronto

The McGraw·Hill Companies

Library of Congress Cataloging-in-Publication Data

Resumes for high school graduates / the editors of McGraw-Hill.—3rd ed.
p.   cm. — (McGraw-Hill professional resumes series)
ISBN 0-07-144891-8 (alk. paper)
1. Resumes (Employment)   2. High school graduates—Employment—United
States.   I. McGraw-Hill Companies.   II. Series.

HF5383.R438   2006
650.14'2—dc22   2005042597

2 3 4 5 6 7 8 9 0   QPD/QPD   0 9 8 7 6

ISBN 0-07-144891-8

McGraw-Hill books are available at special quantity discounts to use as premiums and sales promotions, or for use in corporate training programs. For more information, please write to the Director of Special Sales, Professional Publishing, McGraw-Hill, Two Penn Plaza, New York, NY 10121-2298. Or contact your local bookstore.

This book is printed on acid-free paper.

Contents

Introduction   *v*

Chapter 1
The Elements of an Effective Resume   *1*

Chapter 2
Writing Your Resume   *17*

Chapter 3
Assembly and Layout   *21*

Chapter 4
The Cover Letter   *33*

Chapter 5
Sample Resumes   *37*

Chapter 6
Sample Cover Letters   *153*

Introduction

Your resume is a piece of paper (or an electronic document) that serves to introduce you to the people who will eventually hire you. To write a thoughtful resume, you must thoroughly assess your personality, your accomplishments, and the skills you have acquired. The act of composing and submitting a resume also requires you to carefully consider the company or individual that might hire you. What are they looking for, and how can you meet their needs? This book shows you how to organize your personal information and experience into a concise and well-written resume so that your qualifications and potential as an employee will be understood easily and quickly by a complete stranger.

Writing the resume is just one step in what can be a daunting job-search process, but it is an important element in the chain of events that will lead you to your new position. While you are probably a talented, bright, and charming person, your resume may not reflect these qualities. A poorly written resume can get you nowhere; a well-written resume can land you an interview and potentially a job. A good resume can even lead the interviewer to ask you questions that will allow you to talk about your strengths and highlight the skills you can bring to a prospective employer. Even a person with very little experience can find a good job if he or she is assisted by a thoughtful and polished resume.

Lengthy, typewritten resumes are a thing of the past. Today, employers do not have the time or the patience for verbose documents; they look for tightly composed, straightforward, action-based resumes. Although a one-page resume is the norm, a two-page resume may be warranted if you have had extensive job experience or have changed careers and truly need the space to properly position yourself. If, after careful editing, you still need more than one page to present yourself, it's acceptable to use a second page. A crowded resume that's hard to read would be the worst of your choices.

Distilling your work experience, education, and interests into such a small space requires preparation and thought. This book takes you step-by-step through the process of crafting an effective resume that will stand out in today's competitive marketplace. It serves as a workbook and a place to write down your experiences, while also including the techniques you'll need to pull all the necessary elements together. In the following pages, you'll find many examples of resumes that are specific to your area of interest. Study them for inspiration and find what appeals to you. There are a variety of ways to organize and present your information; inside, you'll find several that will be suitable to your needs. Good luck landing the job of your dreams!

Chapter 1

The Elements of an Effective Resume

An effective resume is composed of information that employers are most interested in knowing about a prospective job applicant. This information is conveyed by a few essential elements. The following is a list of elements that are found in most resumes—some essential, some optional. Later in this chapter, we will further examine the role of each of these elements in the makeup of your resume.

- Heading
- Objective and/or Keyword Section
- Work Experience
- Education
- Honors
- Activities
- Certificates and Licenses
- Publications
- Professional Memberships
- Special Skills
- Personal Information
- References

The first step in preparing your resume is to gather information about yourself and your past accomplishments. Later you will refine this information, rewrite it using effective language, and organize it into an attractive layout. But first, let's take a look at each of these important elements individually so you can judge their appropriateness for your resume.

Heading

Although the heading may seem to be the simplest section of your resume, be careful not to take it lightly. It is the first section your prospective employer will see, and it contains the information she or he will need to contact you. At the very least, the heading must contain your name, your home address, and, of course, a phone number where you can be reached easily.

In today's high-tech world, many of us have multiple ways that we can be contacted. You may list your e-mail address if you are reasonably sure the employer makes use of this form of communication. Keep in mind, however, that others may have access to your e-mail messages if you send them from an account provided by your current company. If this is a concern, do not list your work e-mail address on your resume. If you are able to take calls at your current place of business, you should include your work number, because most employers will attempt to contact you during typical business hours.

If you have voice mail or a reliable answering machine at home or at work, list its number in the heading and make sure your greeting is professional and clear. Always include at least one phone number in your heading, even if it is a temporary number, where a prospective employer can leave a message.

You might have a dozen different ways to be contacted, but you do not need to list all of them. Confine your numbers or addresses to those that are the easiest for the prospective employer to use and the simplest for you to retrieve.

Objective

When seeking a specific career path, it is important to list a job or career objective on your resume. This statement helps employers know the direction you see yourself taking, so they can determine whether your goals are in line with those of their organization and the position available. Normally, an objective is one to two sentences long. Its contents will vary depending on your career field, goals, and personality. The objective can be specific or general, but it should always be to the point. See the sample resumes in this book for examples.

If you are planning to use this resume online, or you suspect your potential employer is likely to scan your resume, you will want to include a "keyword" in the objective. This allows a prospective employer, searching hundreds of resumes for a specific skill or position objective, to locate the keyword and find your resume. In essence, a keyword is what's "hot" in your particular field at a given time. It's a buzzword, a shorthand way of getting a particular message across at a glance. For example, if you are a lawyer, your objective might state your desire to work in the area of corporate litigation. In this case, someone searching for the keyword "corporate litigation" will pull up your resume and know that you want to plan, research, and present cases at trial on behalf of the corporation. If your objective states that you "desire a challenging position in systems design," the keyword is "systems design," an industry-specific shorthand way of saying that you want to be involved in assessing the need for, acquiring, and implementing high-technology systems. These are keywords and every industry has them, so it's becoming more and more important to include a few in your resume. (You may need to conduct additional research to make sure you know what keywords are most likely to be used in your desired industry, profession, or situation.)

There are many resume and job-search sites online. Like most things in the online world, they vary a great deal in quality. Use your discretion. If you plan to apply for jobs online or advertise your availability this way, you will want to design a scannable resume. This type of resume uses a format that can be easily scanned into a computer and added to a database. Scanning allows a prospective employer to use keywords to quickly review each applicant's experience and skills, and (in the event that there are many candidates for the job) to keep your resume for future reference.

Many people find that it is worthwhile to create two or more versions of their basic resume. You may want an intricately designed resume on high-quality paper to mail or hand out *and* a resume that is designed to be scanned into a computer and saved on a database or an online job site. You can even create a resume in ASCII text to e-mail to prospective employers. For further information, you may wish to refer to the *Guide to Internet Job Searching*, by Frances Roehm and Margaret Dikel, updated and published every other year by McGraw-Hill. This excellent book contains helpful and detailed information about formatting a resume for Internet use. To get you started, in Chapter 3 we have included a list of things to keep in mind when creating electronic resumes.

Although it is usually a good idea to include an objective, in some cases this element is not necessary. The goal of the objective statement is to provide the employer with an idea of where you see yourself going in the field. However, if you are uncertain of the exact nature of the job you seek, including an objective that is too specific could result in your not being considered for a host of perfectly acceptable positions. If you decide not to use an objective heading in your resume, you should definitely incorporate the information that would be conveyed in the objective into your cover letter.

Work Experience

Work experience is arguably the most important element of them all. Unless you are a recent graduate or former homemaker with little or no relevant work experience, your current and former positions will provide the central focus of the resume. You will want this section to be as complete and carefully constructed as possible. By thoroughly examining your work experience, you can get to the heart of your accomplishments and present them in a way that demonstrates and highlights your qualifications.

If you are just entering the workforce, your resume will probably focus on your education, but you should also include information on your work or volunteer experiences. Although you will have less information about work experience than a person who has held multiple positions or is advanced in his or her career, the amount of information is not what is most important in this section. How the information is presented and what it says about you as a worker and a person are what really count.

As you create this section of your resume, remember the need for accuracy. Include all the necessary information about each of your jobs, including your job title, dates of employment, name of your employer, city, state, responsibilities, special projects you handled, and accomplishments. Be sure to list only accomplishments for which you were directly responsible. And don't be alarmed if you haven't participated in or worked on special projects, because this section may not be relevant to certain jobs.

The most common way to list your work experience is in *reverse chronological order*. In other words, start with your most recent job and work your way backward. This way, your prospective employer sees your current (and often most important) position before considering your past employment. Your most recent position, if it's the most important in terms of responsibilities and relevance to the job for which you are applying, should also be the one that includes the most information as compared to your previous positions.

Even if the work itself seems unrelated to your proposed career path, you should list any job or experience that will help sell your talents. If you were promoted or given greater responsibilities or commendations, be sure to mention the fact.

The following worksheet is provided to help you organize your experiences in the working world. It will also serve as an excellent resource to refer to when updating your resume in the future.

WORK EXPERIENCE

Job One:

Job Title _____

Dates _____

Employer _____

City, State _____

Major Duties _____

_____

_____

_____

_____

_____

_____

_____

_____

Special Projects _____

_____

_____

_____

Accomplishments _____

_____

_____

_____

_____

_____

Job Two:

Job Title _____

Dates _____

Employer _____

City, State _____

Major Duties _____

_____

_____

_____

_____

_____

_____

_____

Special Projects _____

_____

_____

_____

Accomplishments _____

_____

_____

_____

_____

_____

_____

_____

Job Three:

Job Title _____

Dates _____

Employer _____

City, State _____

Major Duties _____

_____

_____

_____

_____

_____

_____

_____

Special Projects _____

_____

_____

_____

Accomplishments _____

_____

_____

_____

_____

_____

_____

_____

Job Four:

Job Title _____

Dates _____

Employer _____

City, State _____

Major Duties _____

_____

_____

_____

_____

_____

_____

_____

_____

Special Projects _____

_____

_____

_____

Accomplishments _____

_____

_____

_____

_____

_____

_____

_____

Education

Education is usually the second most important element of a resume. Your educational background is often a deciding factor in an employer's decision to interview you. Highlight your accomplishments in school as much as you did those accomplishments at work. If you are looking for your first professional job, your education or life experience will be your greatest asset because your related work experience will be minimal. In this case, the education section becomes the most important means of selling yourself.

Include in this section all the degrees or certificates you have received; your major or area of concentration; all of the honors you earned; and any relevant activities you participated in, organized, or chaired. Again, list your most recent schooling first. If you have completed graduate-level work, begin with that and work your way back through your undergraduate education. If you have completed college, you generally should not list your high-school experience; do so only if you earned special honors, you had a grade point average that was much better than the norm, or this was your highest level of education.

If you have completed a large number of credit hours in a subject that may be relevant to the position you are seeking but did not obtain a degree, you may wish to list the hours or classes you completed. Keep in mind, however, that you may be asked to explain why you did not finish the program. If you are currently in school, list the degree, certificate, or license you expect to obtain and the projected date of completion.

The following worksheet will help you gather the information you need for this section of your resume.

EDUCATION

School One _____

Major or Area of Concentration _____

Degree _____

Dates _____

School Two _____

Major or Area of Concentration _____

Degree _____

Dates _____

Honors

If you include an honors section in your resume, you should highlight any awards, honors, or memberships in honorary societies that you have received. (You may also incorporate this information into your education section.) Often, the honors are academic in nature, but this section also may be used for special achievements in sports, clubs, or other school activities. Always include the name of the organization awarding the honor and the date(s) received. Use the following worksheet to help you gather your information.

HONORS

Honor One _____

Awarding Organization _____

Date(s) _____

Honor Two _____

Awarding Organization _____

Date(s) _____

Honor Three _____

Awarding Organization _____

Date(s) _____

Honor Four _____

Awarding Organization _____

Date(s) _____

Honor Five _____

Awarding Organization _____

Date(s) _____

Activities

Perhaps you have been active in different organizations or clubs; often an employer will look at such involvement as evidence of initiative, dedication, and good social skills. Examples of your ability to take a leading role in a group should be included on a resume, if you can provide them. The activities section of your resume should present neighborhood and community activities, volunteer positions, and so forth. In general, you may want to avoid listing any organization whose name indicates the race, creed, sex, age, marital status, sexual orientation, or nation of origin of its members because this could expose you to discrimination. Use the following worksheet to list the specifics of your activities.

ACTIVITIES

Organization/Activity _____

Accomplishments _____

_____

_____

Organization/Activity _____

Accomplishments _____

_____

_____

Organization/Activity _____

Accomplishments _____

_____

_____

As your work experience grows through the years, your school activities and honors will carry less weight and be emphasized less in your resume. Eventually, you will probably list only your degree and any major honors received. As time goes by, your job performance and the experience you've gained become the most important elements in your resume, which should change to reflect this.

Certificates and Licenses

If your chosen career path requires specialized training, you may already have certificates or licenses. You should list these if the job you are seeking requires them and you, of course, have acquired them. If you have applied for a license but have not yet received it, use the phrase "application pending."

License requirements vary by state. If you have moved or are planning to relocate to another state, check with that state's board or licensing agency for all licensing requirements.

Always make sure that all of the information you list is completely accurate. Locate copies of your certificates and licenses, and check the exact date and name of the accrediting agency. Use the following worksheet to organize the necessary information.

CERTIFICATES AND LICENSES

Name of License _____

Licensing Agency _____

Date Issued _____

Name of License _____

Licensing Agency _____

Date Issued _____

Name of License _____

Licensing Agency _____

Date Issued _____

Publications

Some professions strongly encourage or even require that you publish. If you have written, coauthored, or edited any books, articles, professional papers, or works of a similar nature that pertain to your field, you will definitely want to include this element. Remember to list the date of publication and the publisher's name, and specify whether you were the sole author or a coauthor. Book, magazine, or journal titles are generally italicized, while the titles of articles within a larger publication appear in quotes. (Check with your reference librarian for more about the appropriate way to present this information.) For scientific or research papers, you will need to give the date, place, and audience to whom the paper was presented.

Use the following worksheet to help you gather the necessary information about your publications.

PUBLICATIONS

Title and Type (Note, Article, etc.) _____

Title of Publication (Journal, Book, etc.) _____

Publisher _____

Date Published _____

Title and Type (Note, Article, etc.) _____

Title of Publication (Journal, Book, etc.) _____

Publisher _____

Date Published _____

Title and Type (Note, Article, etc.) _____

Title of Publication (Journal, Book, etc.) _____

Publisher _____

Date Published _____

Professional Memberships

Another potential element in your resume is a section listing professional memberships. Use this section to describe your involvement in professional associations, unions, and similar organizations. It is to your advantage to list any professional memberships that pertain to the job you are seeking. Many employers see your membership as representative of your desire to stay up-to-date and connected in your field. Include the dates of your involvement and whether you took part in any special activities or held any offices within the organization. Use the following worksheet to organize your information.

PROFESSIONAL MEMBERSHIPS

Name of Organization _____

Office(s) Held_____

Activities _____

Dates _____

Name of Organization _____

Office(s) Held_____

Activities _____

Dates _____

Name of Organization _____

Office(s) Held_____

Activities _____

Dates _____

Name of Organization _____

Office(s) Held_____

Activities _____

Dates _____

Special Skills

The special skills section of your resume is the place to mention any special abilities you have that relate to the job you are seeking. You can use this element to present certain talents or experiences that are not necessarily a part of your education or work experience. Common examples include fluency in a foreign language, extensive travel abroad, or knowledge of a particular computer application. "Special skills" can encompass a wide range of talents, and this section can be used creatively. However, for each skill you list, you should be able to describe how it would be a direct asset in the type of work you're seeking because employers may ask just that in an interview. If you can't think of a way to do this, it may be extraneous information.

Personal Information

Some people include personal information on their resumes. This is generally not recommended, but you might wish to include it if you think that something in your personal life, such as a hobby or talent, has some bearing on the position you are seeking. This type of information is often referred to at the beginning of an interview, when it may be used as an icebreaker. Of course, personal information regarding your age, marital status, race, religion, or sexual orientation should never appear on your resume as personal information. It should be given only in the context of memberships and activities, and only when doing so would not expose you to discrimination.

References

References are not usually given on the resume itself, but a prospective employer needs to know that you have references who may be contacted if necessary. All you need to include is a single sentence at the end of the resume: "References are available upon request," or even simply, "References available." Have a reference list ready—your interviewer may ask to see it! Contact each person on the list ahead of time to see whether it is all right for you to use him or her as a reference. This way, the person has a chance to think about what to say *before* the call occurs. This helps ensure that you will obtain the best reference possible.

Chapter 2

Writing Your Resume

Now that you have gathered the information for each section of your resume, it's time to write it out in a way that will get the attention of the reviewer—hopefully, your future employer! The language you use in your resume will affect its success, so you must be careful and conscientious. Translate the facts you have gathered into the active, precise language of resume writing. You will be aiming for a resume that keeps the reader's interest and highlights your accomplishments in a concise and effective way.

Resume writing is unlike any other form of writing. Although your seventh-grade composition teacher would not approve, the rules of punctuation and sentence building are often completely ignored. Instead, you should try for a functional, direct writing style that focuses on the use of verbs and other words that imply action on your part. Writing with action words and strong verbs characterizes you to potential employers as an energetic, active person, someone who completes tasks and achieves results from his or her work. Resumes that do not make use of action words can sound passive and stale. These resumes are not effective and do not get the attention of any employer, no matter how qualified the applicant. Choose words that display your strengths and demonstrate your initiative. The following list of commonly used verbs will help you create a strong resume:

administered	assembled
advised	assumed responsibility
analyzed	billed
arranged	built

carried out	inspected
channeled	interviewed
collected	introduced
communicated	invented
compiled	maintained
completed	managed
conducted	met with
contacted	motivated
contracted	negotiated
coordinated	operated
counseled	orchestrated
created	ordered
cut	organized
designed	oversaw
determined	performed
developed	planned
directed	prepared
dispatched	presented
distributed	produced
documented	programmed
edited	published
established	purchased
expanded	recommended
functioned as	recorded
gathered	reduced
handled	referred
hired	represented
implemented	researched
improved	reviewed

saved	supervised
screened	taught
served as	tested
served on	trained
sold	typed
suggested	wrote

Let's look at two examples that differ only in their writing style. The first resume section is ineffective because it does not use action words to accent the applicant's work experiences.

WORK EXPERIENCE
Regional Sales Manager

Manager of sales representatives from seven states. Manager of twelve food chain accounts in the East. In charge of the sales force's planned selling toward specific goals. Supervisor and trainer of new sales representatives. Consulting for customers in the areas of inventory management and quality control.

Special Projects: Coordinator and sponsor of annual Food-Industry Seminar.

Accomplishments: Monthly regional volume went up 25 percent during my tenure while, at the same time, a proper sales/cost ratio was maintained. Customer-company relations were improved.

In the following paragraph, we have rewritten the same section using action words. Notice how the tone has changed. It now sounds stronger and more active. This person accomplished goals and really *did* things.

WORK EXPERIENCE
Regional Sales Manager

Managed sales representatives from seven states. Oversaw twelve food chain accounts in the eastern United States. Directed the sales force in planned selling toward specific goals. Supervised and trained new sales representatives. Counseled customers in the areas of inventory management and quality control. Coordinated and sponsored the annual Food Industry Seminar. Increased monthly regional volume by 25 percent and helped to improve customer-company relations during my tenure.

One helpful way to construct the work experience section is to make use of your actual job descriptions—the written duties and expectations your employers have for a person in your current or former position. Job descriptions are rarely written in proper resume language, so you will have to rework them, but they do include much of the information necessary to create this section of your resume. If you have access to job descriptions for your former positions, you can use the details to construct an action-oriented paragraph. Often, your human resources department can provide a job description for your current position.

The following is an example of a typical human resources job description, followed by a rewritten version of the same description employing action words and specific details about the job. Again, pay attention to the style of writing instead of the content, as the details of your own experience will be unique.

WORK EXPERIENCE
Public Administrator I

Responsibilities: Coordinate and direct public services to meet the needs of the nation, state, or community. Analyze problems; work with special committees and public agencies; recommend solutions to governing bodies.

Aptitudes and Skills: Ability to relate to and communicate with people; solve complex problems through analysis; plan, organize, and implement policies and programs. Knowledge of political systems, financial management, personnel administration, program evaluation, and organizational theory.

WORK EXPERIENCE
Public Administrator I

Wrote pamphlets and conducted discussion groups to inform citizens of legislative processes and consumer issues. Organized and supervised 25 interviewers. Trained interviewers in effective communication skills.

After you have written out your resume, you are ready to begin the next important step: assembly and layout.

Assembly and Layout

At this point, you've gathered all the necessary information for your resume and rewritten it in language that will impress your potential employers. Your next step is to assemble the sections in a logical order and lay them out on the page neatly and attractively to achieve the desired effect: getting the interview.

Assembly

The order of the elements in a resume makes a difference in its overall effect. Clearly, you would not want to bury your name and address somewhere in the middle of the resume. Nor would you want to lead with a less important section, such as special skills. Put the elements in an order that stresses your most important accomplishments and the things that will be most appealing to your potential employer. For example, if you are new to the workforce, you will want the reviewer to read about your education and life skills before any part-time jobs you may have held for short durations. On the other hand, if you have been gainfully employed for several years and currently hold an important position in your company, you should list your work accomplishments ahead of your educational information, which has become less pertinent with time.

Certain things should always be included in your resume, but others are optional. The following list shows you which are which. You might want to use it as a checklist to be certain that you have included all of the necessary information.

Essential	**Optional**
Name	Cellular Phone Number
Address	Pager Number
Phone Number	E-Mail Address or Website Address
Work Experience	Voice Mail Number
Education	Job Objective
References Phrase	Honors
	Special Skills
	Publications
	Professional Memberships
	Activities
	Certificates and Licenses
	Personal Information
	Graphics
	Photograph

Your choice of optional sections depends on your own background and employment needs. Always use information that will put you in a favorable light—unless it's absolutely essential, avoid anything that will prompt the interviewer to ask questions about your weaknesses or something else that could be unflattering. Make sure your information is accurate and truthful. If your honors are impressive, include them in the resume. If your activities in school demonstrate talents that are necessary for the job you are seeking, allow space for a section on activities. If you are applying for a position that requires ornamental illustration, you may want to include border illustrations or graphics that demonstrate your talents in this area. If you are answering an advertisement for a job that requires certain physical traits, a photo of yourself might be appropriate. A person applying for a job as a computer programmer would *not* include a photo as part of his or her resume. Each resume is unique, just as each person is unique.

Types of Resumes

So far we have focused on the most common type of resume—the *reverse chronological* resume—in which your most recent job is listed first. This is the type of resume usually preferred by those who have to read a large number of resumes, and it is by far the most popular and widely circulated. However, this style of presentation may not be the most effective way to highlight *your* skills and accomplishments.

For example, if you are reentering the workforce after many years or are trying to change career fields, the *functional* resume may work best. This type of resume puts the focus on your achievements instead of the sequence of your work history. In the functional resume, your experience is presented through your general accomplishments and the skills you have developed in your working life.

A functional resume is assembled from the same information you gathered in Chapter 1. The main difference lies in how you organize the information. Essentially, the work experience section is divided in two, with your job duties and accomplishments constituting one section and your employers' names, cities, and states; your positions; and the dates employed making up the other. Place the first section near the top of your resume, just below your job objective (if used), and call it *Accomplishments* or *Achievements*. The second section, containing the bare essentials of your work history, should come after the accomplishments section and can be called *Employment History*, since it is a chronological overview of your former jobs.

The other sections of your resume remain the same. The work experience section is the only one affected in the functional format. By placing the section that focuses on your achievements at the beginning, you draw attention to these achievements. This puts less emphasis on where you worked and when, and more on what you did and what you are capable of doing.

If you are changing careers, the emphasis on skills and achievements is important. The identities of previous employers (who aren't part of your new career field) need to be downplayed. A functional resume can help accomplish this task. If you are reentering the workforce after a long absence, a functional resume is the obvious choice. And if you lack full-time work experience, you will need to draw attention away from this fact and put the focus on your skills and abilities. You may need to highlight your volunteer activities and part-time work. Education may also play a more important role in your resume.

The type of resume that is right for you will depend on your personal circumstances. It may be helpful to create both types and then compare them. Which one presents you in the best light? Examples of both types of resumes are included in this book. Use the sample resumes in Chapter 5 to help you decide on the content, presentation, and look of your own resume.

Resume or Curriculum Vitae?

A curriculum vitae (CV) is a longer, more detailed synopsis of your professional history, which generally runs three or more pages in length. It includes a summary of your educational and academic background as well as teaching and research experience, publications, presentations, awards, honors, affiliations, and other details. Because the purpose of the CV is different from that of the resume, many of the rules we've discussed thus far involving style and length do not apply.

A curriculum vitae is used primarily for admissions applications to graduate or professional schools, independent consulting in a variety of settings, proposals for fellowships or grants, or applications for positions in academia. As with a resume, you may need different versions of a CV for different types of positions. You should only send a CV when one is specifically requested by an employer or institution.

Like a resume, your CV should include your name, contact information, education, skills, and experience. In addition to the basics, a CV includes research and teaching experience, publications, grants and fellowships, professional associations and licenses, awards, and other information relevant to the position for which you are applying. You can follow the advice presented thus far to gather and organize your personal information.

Special Tips for Electronic Resumes

Because there are many details to consider in writing a resume that will be posted or transmitted on the Internet, or one that will be scanned into a computer when it is received, we suggest that you refer to the *Guide to Internet Job Searching*, by Frances Roehm and Margaret Dikel, as previously mentioned. However, here are some brief, general guidelines to follow if you expect your resume to be scanned into a computer.

- Use standard fonts in which none of the letters touch.

- Keep in mind that underlining, italics, and fancy scripts may not scan well.

- Use boldface and capitalization to set off elements. Again, make sure letters don't touch. Leave at least a quarter inch between lines of type.

- Keep information and elements at the left margin. Centering, columns, and even indenting may change when the resume is optically scanned.

- Do not use any lines, boxes, or graphics.

- Place the most important information at the top of the first page. If you use two pages, put "Page 1 of 2" at the bottom of the first page and put your name and "Page 2 of 2" at the top of the second page.

- List each telephone number on its own line in the header.

- Use multiple keywords or synonyms for what you do to make sure your qualifications will be picked up if a prospective employer is searching for them. Use nouns that are keywords for your profession.

- Be descriptive in your titles. For example, don't just use "assistant"; use "legal office assistant."

- Make sure the contrast between print and paper is good. Use a high-quality laser printer and white or very light colored 8½-by-11-inch paper.

- Mail a high-quality laser print or an excellent copy. Do not fold or use staples, as this might interfere with scanning. You may, however, use paper clips.

In addition to creating a resume that works well for scanning, you may want to have a resume that can be e-mailed to reviewers. Because you may not know what word processing application the recipient uses, the best format to use is ASCII text. (ASCII stands for "American Standard Code for Information Interchange.") It allows people with very different software platforms to exchange and understand information. (E-mail operates on this principle.) ASCII is a simple, text-only language, which means you can include only simple text. There can be no use of boldface, italics, or even paragraph indentations.

To create an ASCII resume, just use your normal word processing program; when finished, save it as a "text only" document. You will find this option under the "save" or "save as" command. Here is a list of things to *avoid* when crafting your electronic resume:

- Tabs. Use your space bar. Tabs will not work.

- Any special characters, such as mathematical symbols.

- Word wrap. Use hard returns (the return key) to make line breaks.

- Centering or other formatting. Align everything at the left margin.

- Bold or italic fonts. Everything will be converted to plain text when you save the file as a "text only" document.

Check carefully for any mistakes before you save the document as a text file. Spellcheck and proofread it several times; then ask someone with a keen eye to go over it again for you. Remember: the key is to keep it simple. Any attempt to make this resume pretty or decorative may result in a resume that is confusing and hard to read. After you have saved the document, you can cut and paste it into an e-mail or onto a website.

Layout for a Paper Resume

A great deal of care—and much more formatting—is necessary to achieve an attractive layout for your paper resume. There is no single appropriate layout that applies to every resume, but there are a few basic rules to follow in putting your resume on paper:

- Leave a comfortable margin on the sides, top, and bottom of the page (usually one to one and a half inches).

- Use appropriate spacing between the sections (two to three line spaces are usually adequate).

- Be consistent in the *type* of headings you use for different sections of your resume. For example, if you capitalize the heading EMPLOYMENT HISTORY, don't use initial capitals and underlining for a section of equal importance, such as Education.

- Do not use more than one font in your resume. Stay consistent by choosing a font that is fairly standard and easy to read, and don't change it for different sections. Beware of the tendency to try to make your resume original by choosing fancy type styles; your resume may end up looking unprofessional instead of creative. Unless you are in a very creative and artistic field, you should almost always stick with tried-and-true type styles like Times New Roman and Palatino, which are often used in business writing. In the area of resume styles, conservative is usually the best way to go.

CHRONOLOGICAL RESUME

Jennifer Rosales

381 Ponderosa Avenue • Albuquerque, NM 87198
(505) 555-3578 • jennifer.rosales@xxx.com

GOAL

A position that utilizes my strong organizational and multitasking skills.

WORK EXPERIENCE

August 2004 to May 2005
Food Service Worker. Kentucky Fried Chicken, Albuquerque, NM.
Responsibilities: Taking and preparing food orders, running cash register, stocking supplies, and cleaning kitchen and eating areas.

May 2004 to August 2004
Receptionist. Santa Fe Real Estate Company, Albuquerque, NM.
Responsibilities: Answering phones and calling customers for further information pertaining to their homes. Maintaining client contacts via Microsoft Office Outlook.

Prior to May 2004
Babysitter.

OTHER EXPERIENCE

- I am a student in O.W.E., "Outside Work Experience," learning about jobs and future careers.
- I am fluent in Spanish.
- I was a volunteer camp counselor working with children aged 11 to 13, assisting with sports and recreational activities.
- I was a member of the following Albuquerque High School groups: Unity Among Us, Students in Christian Fellowship, Student Body Council, and Going Places Academically.
- I am involved with church activities.

EDUCATION

I am a graduate of Albuquerque High School, 2004.
My future educational plans are to attend Albuquerque Technical and Vocational Institute.

REFERENCES

Available upon request.

FUNCTIONAL RESUME

MICHAEL SUTHERLAND
2757 Dolphin Dr. • Arnold, MD 21012 • (301) 555-5390 • michael.sutherland@xxx.com

OBJECTIVE
A part-time position as an usher

EDUCATION
UCLA School of Theater, Film, and TV, beginning Fall 2004
Comprehensive Major: Directing and Theater Management

Arnold High School, June 2004
Forensics Competitive Speech Team (four years)
Drama and Musical Productions (three years)

AWARDS
- Bank of Maryland Fine Arts Award—2nd place, Region Finals Scholarship, 2004
- Veterans of Foreign Wars Speech Award, 2003 and 2004
- Student of the Year—Arnold High School, 2003
- Boys' State Delegate, 2003
- State Forensics for Thematic Interpretation, 21st place (Pieces included: *Torch Song Trilogy*, *Into the Woods*, *Brighton Beach Memoirs*, *Measure for Measure*), 2003
- Rotary Speech Award, 2001 and 2002
- Walter Johnson Musical Comedy Award at Anne Arundel Community Stage, 2001

PERFORMANCE THEATER EXPERIENCE
Director, Collaborator, and Performer, AIDS Teen Theater, 2004
"Billy Crocker" in *Anything Goes*, 2003
"Vincentio" in *Taming of the Shrew*, 2003
"Albert" in *Bye-Bye Birdie*, 2002
"Frank Butler" in *Annie Get Your Gun*, 2001
"Charlie" in *Charlie and the Chocolate Factory*, 2001

TECHNICAL AND MANAGING THEATER EXPERIENCE
Anne Arundel Community Stage
Production Assistant—*Fiddler on the Roof*, 2004
Assistant Stage Manager—*Into the Woods*, 2002
Assistant Stage Manager—*Camelot*, 2001
Chorus and Stagehand—*Evita*, 2000
Stagehand—*My Fair Lady*, 2000

REFERENCES
Available upon request

- Always try to fit your resume on one page. If you are having trouble with this, you may be trying to say too much. Edit out any repetitive or unnecessary information, and shorten descriptions of earlier jobs where possible. Ask a friend you trust for feedback on what seems unnecessary or unimportant. For example, you may have included too many optional sections. Today, with the prevalence of the personal computer as a tool, there is no excuse for a poorly laid out resume. Experiment with variations until you are pleased with the result.

Remember that a resume is not an autobiography. Too much information will only get in the way. The more compact your resume, the easier it will be to review. If a person who is swamped with resumes looks at yours, catches the main points, and then calls you for an interview to fill in some of the details, your resume has already accomplished its task. A clear and concise resume makes for a happy reader and a good impression.

There are times when, despite extensive editing, the resume simply cannot fit on one page. In this case, the resume should be laid out on two pages in such a way that neither clarity nor appearance is compromised. Each page of a two-page resume should be marked clearly: the first should indicate "Page 1 of 2," and the second should include your name and the page number, for example, "Julia Ramirez—Page 2 of 2." The pages should then be paper-clipped together. You may use a smaller type size (in the same font as the body of your resume) for the page numbers. Place them at the bottom of page one and the top of page two. Again, spend the time now to experiment with the layout until you find one that looks good to you.

Always show your final layout to other people and ask them what they like or dislike about it, and what impresses them most when they read your resume. Make sure that their responses are the same as what you want to elicit from your prospective employer. If they aren't the same, you should continue to make changes until the necessary information is emphasized.

Proofreading

After you have finished typing the master copy of your resume and before you have it copied or printed, thoroughly check it for typing and spelling errors. Do not place all your trust in your computer's spellcheck function. Use an old editing trick and read the whole resume backward—start at the end and read it right to left and bottom to top. This can help you see the small errors or inconsistencies that are easy to overlook. Take time to do it right because a single error on a document this important can cause the reader to judge your attention to detail in a harsh light.

Have several people look at the finished resume just in case you've missed an error. Don't try to take a shortcut; not having an unbiased set of eyes examine your resume now could mean embarrassment later. Even experienced editors can easily overlook their own errors. Be thorough and conscientious with your proofreading so your first impression is a perfect one.

We have included the following rules of capitalization and punctuation to assist you in the final stage of creating your resume. Remember that resumes often require use of a shorthand style of writing that may include sentences without periods and other stylistic choices that break the standard rules of grammar. Be consistent in each section and throughout the whole resume with your choices.

RULES OF CAPITALIZATION

- Capitalize proper nouns, such as names of schools, colleges, and universities; names of companies; and brand names of products.

- Capitalize major words in the names and titles of books, tests, and articles that appear in the body of your resume.

- Capitalize words in major section headings of your resume.

- Do not capitalize words just because they seem important.

- When in doubt, consult a style manual such as *Words into Type* (Prentice Hall) or *The Chicago Manual of Style* (The University of Chicago Press). Your local library can help you locate these and other reference books. Many computer programs also have grammar help sections.

RULES OF PUNCTUATION

- Use commas to separate words in a series.

- Use a semicolon to separate series of words that already include commas within the series. (For an example, see the first rule of capitalization.)

- Use a semicolon to separate independent clauses that are not joined by a conjunction.

- Use a period to end a sentence.

- Use a colon to show that examples or details follow that will expand or amplify the preceding phrase.

- Avoid the use of dashes.

- Avoid the use of brackets.

- If you use any punctuation in an unusual way in your resume, be consistent in its use.

- Whenever you are uncertain, consult a style manual.

Putting Your Resume in Print

You will need to buy high-quality paper for your printer before you print your finished resume. Regular office paper is not good enough for resumes; the reviewer will probably think it looks flimsy and cheap. Go to an office supply store or copy shop and select a high-quality bond paper that will make a good first impression. Select colors like white, off-white, or possibly a light gray. In some industries, a pastel may be acceptable, but be sure the color and feel of the paper make a subtle, positive statement about you. Nothing in the choice of paper should be loud or unprofessional.

If your computer printer does not reproduce your resume properly and produces smudged or stuttered type, either ask to borrow a friend's or take your disk (or a clean original) to a printer or copy shop for high-quality copying. If you anticipate needing a large number of copies, taking your resume to a copy shop or a printer is probably the best choice.

Hold a sheet of your unprinted bond paper up to the light. If it has a watermark, you will want to point this out to the person helping you with copies; the printing should be done so that the reader can read the print and see the watermark the right way up. Check each copy for smudges or streaks. This is the time to be a perfectionist—the results of your careful preparation will be well worth it.

Chapter 4

The Cover Letter

Once your resume has been assembled, laid out, and printed to your satisfaction, the next and final step before distribution is to write your cover letter. Though there may be instances where you deliver your resume in person, you will usually send it through the mail or online. Resumes sent through the mail always need an accompanying letter that briefly introduces you and your resume. The purpose of the cover letter is to get a potential employer to read your resume, just as the purpose of the resume is to get that same potential employer to call you for an interview.

Like your resume, your cover letter should be clean, neat, and direct. A cover letter usually includes the following information:

1. Your name and address (unless it already appears on your personal letterhead) and your phone number(s); see item 7.

2. The date.

3. The name and address of the person and company to whom you are sending your resume.

4. The salutation ("Dear Mr." or "Dear Ms." followed by the person's last name, or "To Whom It May Concern" if you are answering a blind ad).

5. An opening paragraph explaining why you are writing (for example, in response to an ad, as a follow-up to a previous meeting, at the suggestion of someone you both know) and indicating that you are interested in whatever job is being offered.

6. One or more paragraphs that tell why you want to work for the company and what qualifications and experiences you can bring to the position. This is a good place to mention some detail about

that particular company that makes you want to work for them; this shows that you have done some research before applying.

7. A final paragraph that closes the letter and invites the reviewer to contact you for an interview. This can be a good place to tell the potential employer which method would be best to use when contacting you. Be sure to give the correct phone number and a good time to reach you, if that is important. You may mention here that your references are available upon request.

8. The closing ("Sincerely" or "Yours truly") followed by your signature in a dark ink, with your name typed under it.

Your cover letter should include all of this information and be no longer than one page in length. The language used should be polite, businesslike, and to the point. Don't attempt to tell your life story in the cover letter; a long and cluttered letter will serve only to annoy the reader. Remember that you need to mention only a few of your accomplishments and skills in the cover letter. The rest of your information is available in your resume. If your cover letter is a success, your resume will be read and all pertinent information reviewed by your prospective employer.

Producing the Cover Letter

Cover letters should always be individualized because they are always written to specific individuals and companies. Never use a form letter for your cover letter or copy it as you would a resume. Each cover letter should be unique, and as personal and lively as possible. (Of course, once you have written and rewritten your first cover letter until you are satisfied with it, you can certainly use similar wording in subsequent letters. You may want to save a template on your computer for future reference.) Keep a hard copy of each cover letter so you know exactly what you wrote in each one.

There are sample cover letters in Chapter 6. Use them as models or for ideas of how to assemble and lay out your own cover letters. Remember that every letter is unique and depends on the particular circumstances of the individual writing it and the job for which he or she is applying.

After you have written your cover letter, proofread it as thoroughly as you did your resume. Again, spelling or punctuation errors are a sure sign of carelessness, and you don't want that to be a part of your first impression on a prospective employer. This is no time to trust your spellcheck function. Even after going through a spelling and grammar check, your cover letter should be carefully proofread by at least one other person.

Print the cover letter on the same quality bond paper you used for your resume. Remember to sign it, using a good dark-ink pen. Handle the letter and resume carefully to avoid smudging or wrinkling, and mail them together in an appropriately sized envelope. Many stores sell matching envelopes to coordinate with your choice of bond paper.

Keep an accurate record of all resumes you send out and the results of each mailing. This record can be kept on your computer, in a calendar or notebook, or on file cards. Knowing when a resume is likely to have been received will keep you on track as you make follow-up phone calls.

About a week after mailing resumes and cover letters to potential employers, contact them by telephone. Confirm that your resume arrived and ask whether an interview might be possible. Be sure to record the name of the person you spoke to and any other information you gleaned from the conversation. It is wise to treat the person answering the phone with a great deal of respect; sometimes the assistant or receptionist has the ear of the person doing the hiring.

You should make a great impression with the strong, straightforward resume and personalized cover letter you have just created. We wish you every success in securing the career of your dreams!

Chapter 5

Sample Resumes

This chapter contains dozens of sample resumes for people pursuing a wide variety of jobs and careers.

There are many different styles of resumes in terms of graphic layout and presentation of information. These samples represent people with varying amounts of education and experience. Use these samples to model your own resume after. Choose one resume, or borrow elements from several different resumes to help you construct your own.

Andrew G. Meunier

6300 Beasley Road • Jackson, MS 39215
Andy.Meunier@xxx.com • (601) 555-7819

Personal Objective:
Job with automotive repair or body shop

Experience:
Automotive Repair and Body Work
- Knowledge of automotive diagnostic computers
- Assisted with complete exterior repair of six cars
- Familiar with engine repair and rebuilding
- Detail painting specialty
- Interior work on several vans

Home Maintenance
- Provided landscaping maintenance and light carpentry for apartment complex
- Familiar with interior and exterior painting of homes
- Assisted with roofing of one new home and repair on another

Work History:
Handyman, Delta Apartments, 2004–present
2400 Albermarle Road, Jackson, MS
Supervisor: Adrian Florio
Duties: landscape maintenance, carpentry, general repair

Custodian, Alternative Junior High School, 2003–2004
1900 N. State Street, Jackson, MS
Supervisor: Johnson Ableman
Duties: basic janitorial work

Skills & Activities:
- Sign language
- Drawing and painting
- Member of Car Rally Club of Jackson
- Boy Scouts of America (Eagle Scout)

Education:
Wingfield Senior High School, Jackson, MS
Graduated June 2005
Courses: Auto Mechanics, Woodshop, Spanish, AutoCAD, Computer Science

References:
Available on request

Latoya Cook

512 Lynn Road
Excelsior Springs, MO 64024
L.Cook@xxx.com
(816) 555-3225

Goal:

An entry position involving writing and editing.

Experience:

Editor, The Easterly Breeze (student newspaper).

- Wrote series on racial integration programs in Missouri high schools. Series won a state Junior Journalist award in 2004 from the Missouri Association of Newspaper Journalists. One article from the series was published in the MANJ newsletter.
- Write monthly column about student life and issues at East High School.
- Interview teachers and students for personality profile articles for publication in the student newspaper.
- Edit stories written by other students for spelling, grammar, and AP news style.

Reporter, Encounters (student yearbook).

- Wrote articles on sports for publication in yearbook.
- Wrote captions for photographs.
- Assisted staff photographers with taking group photographs.

Education:

East High School, Excelsior Springs, MO
September 2001–June 2004
GPA: 3.75
Pertinent Courses: Journalism, Photography, Honors English (3 years), Introduction to Law, Government, Typing, and Computer Science.

References available on request.

Shawana Udey
2354 S.E. Grand Avenue
Billings, MT 59105
E-mail: Shawana.Udey@xxx.com
Cell: (406) 555-5835

Job Desired
Preschool or day care teaching assistant

Work Experience
Childcare Provider, Faubian Elementary School, June 2003–present
3039 N.E. Sierra Boulevard
Billings, MT
Supervisor: Nancy Toppila, (406) 555-5085
Duties: Perform all aspects of childcare during adult education parenting classes. Supervise children, instruct crafts, provide snacks, and monitor children at play and while napping.

Volunteer, St. Vincent's Hospital, June 2002–present
2915 Twelfth Avenue
Billings, MT
Supervisor: Jamilla de Corazon, R.N., (406) 254-2333
Duties: As a volunteer candy striper provide reading materials, frequently read aloud to patients, visit with patients and assist nurses.

Education
Eagle High School, Billings, MT
September 2001–June 2005
2.79 GPA

Relevant Coursework
• Child Development
• Teacher Assistant
• Home Economics and Nutrition
• Health and Fitness

Related Skills
• CPR and basic emergency first aid certification
• Training in baby-sitting from Yellowstone County Red Cross
• Completion of infant care courses at St. Vincent's Hospital

References
On request

ESTRELLA ANGELINO

2240 W. Yucca Street
Santa Fe, NM 87538
E.Angelino@xxx.com
(505) 555-5121

Objective

Finding a challenging part-time job in sales and customer service with an opportunity for future advancement.

Relevant Coursework

Typing I and II
Office Systems and Procedures
English I, II, and III
Computer Applications I and II
Finance and Accounting I and II
Computer Accounting

Education

Capitol High School, Santa Fe, NM
Graduated: 2004

Work Experience

Square Pan Pizza, Santa Fe, NM
April–December 2004
Responsibilities included greeting customers, processing orders, handling cash, operating the register, answering telephones, cooking, cleaning, and assisting with closing.

The Bite of Santa Fe, Santa Fe, NM
Volunteer, 2002–2004
Served as volunteer for the city's annual weekend celebration of food and music in downtown Santa Fe. Provided customer service to the public, took orders, handled cash, and served ice cream and soft drinks.

St. Vincent de Paul, Santa Fe, NM
Volunteer, 2003–present
Serve food and distribute clothing and supplies to people in need.

References available on request

ALEXANDER HYDE

Rural Route 7, Box 43B • Geneva, Nebraska 68361
Home: (402) 555-2822 • Cell: (402) 555-8105

JOB DESIRED

Bank teller or bank clerk with future opportunities to utilize my education in finance and accounting.

EDUCATION

September 2001–present
Geneva North High School
Geneva, Nebraska

ACHIEVEMENTS

- Completed series of accounting courses that involved recording and analyzing financial transactions, developing financial plans, and preparing financial statements.
- Learned a variety of computer-assisted accounting programs.
- Participated in a simulated business as the financial manager.
- Developed a business plan and worked with the marketing manager to carry out business objectives.
- Participated in career visitations to a variety of financial institutions.

ACTIVITIES

- Vice-President, Future Business Leaders of America
- Member, DECA (marketing club)
- Reporter on student newspaper
- Treasurer, National Honor Society
- German Club

WORK HISTORY

Burger King, Line Cashier, May 2003–present
366 N.W. Frontage
Geneva, Nebraska
Supervisor: Bobbie Mahew, (402) 555-4655
As a line cashier, I greet customers, take orders, prepare food, handle cash, and balance receipts against sales at the end of my shift.
- I have never been late to work or missed a day.
- Chosen as Cashier of the Month, July 2003.

REFERENCES

Available upon request.

Aimee Dykstra

2825 Evans Avenue
Suncook, New Hampshire 03275
E-mail: a.dykstra@xxx.com
Mobile: (212) 555-9941

Professional Goal
Obtain an internship as an assistant to state legislator

Education
Pembroke Academy, 2001–2005
Suncook, New Hampshire
Graduated: 2005

Exeter School for Girls, 1999–2000
Exeter, New Hampshire
   Relevant Courses:
   • American Government
   • Business Law
   • Western Civilization
   • World History
   • Sociology

Work Experience
Briscoe and Havering, Attorneys at Law, June–August 2004
Manchester, New Hampshire
   Duties:
   • Worked with attorneys and legal assistants to gather documentation needed for litigation proceedings
   • Assisted with research, maintained legal library records, and obtained necessary materials from central law library at the college

Skills
• Experienced with computers (Microsoft Office Suite in Mac and PC formats)
• Strong research skills including Internet-based research
• Type 45 wpm

Activities
• Competed in a state competition as a member of Model United Nations (Greece)
• Member of Future Business Leaders of America
• Served as Outdoor School Junior Counselor for three sessions
• Coached Junior Soccer for the Boys & Girls Club of Merrimack County

References
Available on request

PATRICIA FINLEY

351 N. 22nd Street • Las Vegas, NV 89102 • Pat.Finley@xxx.com • (702) 555-1377

GOAL

To obtain an entry-level position in bank or bookkeeping firm.

EDUCATION

Clark Senior High School
4291 Pennwood Avenue, Las Vegas
Graduated: 2005

Courses of Study:
• Completed Math (three years), Accounting II, Computer Systems.
• Currently enrolled in Japanese I and Advanced Algebra, and I serve as a
  Teacher's Assistant.

EXPERIENCE

• Experienced with payroll reports and bookkeeping. Studied federal and state
  payroll tax guidelines and prepared quarterly reports.
• Assumed responsibility for three small-business accounts, maintaining income
  and expense ledgers and providing monthly statements.
• Experienced with general ledger accounting on ACCPAC software.
• Served as Treasurer for the marketing club and was responsible for maintaining
  the sales and expense records for the Student Store.

WORK HISTORY

Finley & Associates, CPA Firm, Las Vegas
Summers 2002–present
• Assist with implementing new software programs.
• Established a streamline filing and information storage system, continue to
  maintain system.
• Coordinate monthly mailings and mail out client correspondence.
• Review billing and search for discrepancies and errors.
• Assist with payroll.

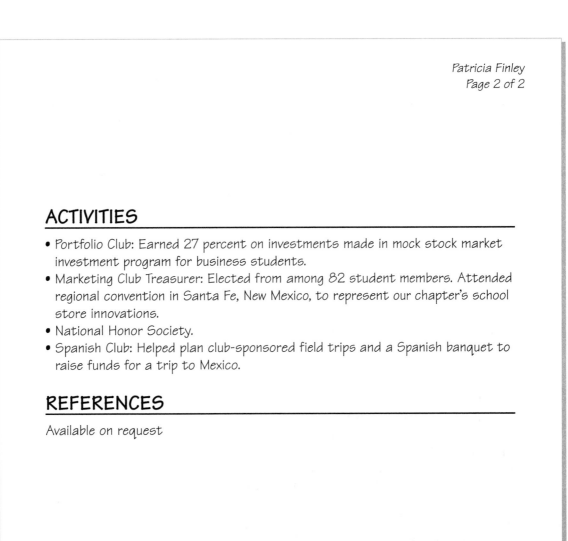

ACTIVITIES

- Portfolio Club: Earned 27 percent on investments made in mock stock market investment program for business students.
- Marketing Club Treasurer: Elected from among 82 student members. Attended regional convention in Santa Fe, New Mexico, to represent our chapter's school store innovations.
- National Honor Society.
- Spanish Club: Helped plan club-sponsored field trips and a Spanish banquet to raise funds for a trip to Mexico.

REFERENCES

Available on request

OMAR HASSAK

288 Palisade Avenue
Jersey City, NJ 07306
Omar.Hassak@xxx.com
(201) 555-2938

JOB DESIRED
Apprentice mechanic with automotive repair company with an opportunity to
train as auto mechanic.

EDUCATION
Dickinson High School, Jersey City, 2003–present
Hudson Regional Junior-Senior High School, Highlands, NJ, 2001–2003

SKILLS
• Mechanically inclined with skills ranging from basic auto mechanics to very
  technical electrical diagnostics.
• Experienced with engine overhaul, suspension, brakes, fuel, power train, and
  motor detailing.
• Some auto-body repair experience.
• Familiar with diesel, electric, and hybrid cars.

WORK EXPERIENCE
Dickinson High School Auto Shop, 2004–present
• Perform tune-ups, oil changes, general check-up, and trouble shooting in
  student run auto mechanics shop.
• Diagnose and repair mechanical problems on cars, trucks, and vans.

East Jersey Radiator, 2004–present
• Clean and test radiators, install replacement radiators, and perform motor
  detailing.
• Shop services both foreign and domestic cars.
• Assisted with stock warehouse.

Northern Landscape Maintenance, 2003–2004
• Planted, mowed, pruned, and trimmed hedges for three apartment complexes
  and four office complexes.
• Maintained nursery inventory.

References available upon request.

JORDAN WILEY
Rural Route 31, Box 243
Cicero, New York 13039
J.Wiley3@xxx.com
(315) 555-2446

JOB OBJECTIVE
Retail sales position

EDUCATION
Cicero-North Syracuse Senior High School
Rural Route 31, Cicero, New York
Graduated: 2005
Related Courses: Accounting I and II, Business Systems, Algebra, and
  Computer Science

Student Training Education Program (STEP)
1421 Stark Street, Syracuse, New York
Related Course: Personal Finance

WORK HISTORY
Chum's Cafe, January 2000–June 2004
204 N.E. Second, Syracuse, New York
Supervisor: Ike Jung, (315) 555-7833

Little Caesar's Restaurant, July 2002–January 2003
1835 N.E. Division, Syracuse, New York
Supervisor: Sandra Pommerville, (315) 555-9025

ACTIVITIES
Offices Held
  • Secretary, Future Business Leaders of America, 2004
  • President, Bike & Hike Club, 2003–2004
Committees
  • Homecoming, 2003–2004
  • Junior and Senior Prom Committee, 2003–2004
Memberships
  • Cub Scouts, 1993–1997
  • Bike & Hike Club, 2002–2005
  • Youth Convention, 2002–2004
  • Syracuse Swiss Sportsman Club, 1991–2003
  • Sports Football, 2000–2004
  • Indoor Track, 2003–2004

References available on request

ARLENE HOSKA

2833 Kennedy Boulevard
Salt Lake City, UT 83902
A.Hoska@xxx.com
Cell: (201) 555-9877

OBJECTIVE

To obtain a position as receptionist for a law office, with a long-range goal of training for advancement to a position as legal secretary.

EDUCATION

St. Michael High School, Salt Lake City, UT
Graduated: 2005
GPA: 3.6
• Courses of Study: Business Law, Typing, Advanced Computers, Marketing, Accounting, and Japanese.

Drake Secretarial College, Salt Lake City, UT
Summer 2004
• Learned shorthand, dictation, and standard business systems.

WORK EXPERIENCE

Receptionist, Law Office of Dupuy, Jakewith, Howard & Taft,
June–August 2004
• Worked as summer replacement receptionist.
• Operated telephone switchboard for an office of eight attorneys, six legal assistants, five legal secretaries, and three law clerks.
• Organized computer mail software installation on all office computers.
• Typed legal documents as needed.

Student Office Assistant, St. Michael High School,
September 2002–June 2004
• Worked in the high school office, answered telephones, greeted visitors, and assisted school secretaries as needed with filing and word processing.
• Maintained daily attendance records for distribution to teachers.

SKILLS

- Strong research skills including Web-based searches.
- Familiar with Microsoft Office including Word, PowerPoint, and Excel.
- Database management background.
- Experience with filing expense reports.
- Ability to operate check register.
- 10-key adding machine.

ACTIVITIES

- Future Business Leaders of America
- Marketing Club
- National Honor Society
- Tennis

REFERENCES

Available on request.

• <u>CARMAN ESPOSITO</u>

2390 N. Harvey, Apt. 4, Richmond, CA 98993
C.Esposito@xxx.com • (503) 555-6870

• OBJECTIVE
Obtain an entry-level position where my organizational and leadership skills can help make a positive difference.

• EDUCATION
Douglas High School, Richmond, CA
Graduated: 2005
GPA: 3.28

• EXPERIENCE & SKILLS DEVELOPMENT
- Promote sales of martial arts merchandise and karate lessons.
- Assist with office operations, answer telephones, schedule lesson times, assist students and clients.
- Expanded computer usage by establishing a customer database and setting up e-mail accounts for employees.
- Teach Kenpo Karate, Thai Boxing, and Freestyle Sparring to children and adults, in both private and group class situations.
- Distribute flyers to individuals on college campuses and in mall parking lots.
- Abilities include sales, telephone communications, computer keyboarding, organization, and customer service.

• WORK HISTORY
Baltimore Kenpo Karate School, Richmond, CA
February 2003–present

• REFERENCES
Available on request.

Kim Gravenstein

111 N.E. 92nd
Lexington, Kentucky 40503
K.Gravenstein@xxx.com
(606) 555-4900

Job Objective

To obtain a part-time secretarial position while attending community college for Accounting.

Education

Bryan Station Senior High School, 2000–2004
Relevant courses of study: Typing, Advanced Algebra, Computer Science, Composition, and Accounting I & II

Work History

Child Care Provider, 2001–present
Rock Creek Lanes, Lexington, Kentucky
Duties: provide quality childcare in playroom and maintain records and billing for childcare

Child Care Provider, 1999–2001
Private individuals, Lexington, Kentucky
Duties: provided full-time summer care for two children in a private home and frequent intermittent evening and weekend care

Office Skills

- Type 50 wpm
- Familiar with both PC and Mac operation systems
- Microsoft Office including Word, PowerPoint, and Excel
- Knowledge of ACT! Database software
- Numerous e-mail systems
- Ability to perform mail merges in Word and ACT!

References

Available on request.

Darien Jackson

1134 N.E. 14th Street
El Dorado, Kansas 67402
E-mail: Darien.Jackson@xxx.com
Cell: (316) 555-3086

Career Goal

My objective is to obtain a position as a forklift operator while I complete college training in engineering and manufacturing.

Education

El Dorado High School
McCullom Road, El Dorado, Kansas
Graduated: June 2005
Courses studied: metal shop, computer applications, woodworking,
                 algebra, and three-dimensional design.

Work Experience

Warehouse Worker; Gates Tire Company, El Dorado, Kansas
June to August 2004
• Assisted with receiving shipments, stocking, and sending shipments.
  Drove forklift and operated loading dock.

Landscape Maintenance; private individuals
June to August 2003
• Planted and removed plants and provided lawn maintenance for a
  variety of personal clients.

Field Worker; Townsend Farms, Inc.
June to August 2002
• Planted and harvested for several crops for small family farm
  operation.

Skills

Able to operate the following machines: lathe, table saw, drill press,
sander, bench grinder, arc welder, and Hyster 2450 forklift.

Activities

• Junior varsity and varsity baseball
• Varsity soccer
• Member of Greater El Dorado Soccer Club
• Computer Club

References

Available on request.

Shelley Tabor

78 N.E. Towbridge Road • Bridgewater, MA 02324
S.Tabor@xxx.com • (508) 555-8281

Objective

Assistant position with preschool or child-care facility.

Education

Bridgewater-Raynham Regional High School
Graduated: 2005
Specialized Courses: Early Childhood Development, Childhood Education/Preschool, Human Development, Preschool Practicum (hands-on experience in the day care/preschool), Health and First Aid.

Relevant Work Experience

Child-care provider for various private individuals, 1999–present
• For two summers, provided full-time care for three children, ages 18 months to 6 years.

Supervisor and Assistant, Girl Scout Troop #475, 2003–present
• Help to organize and plan activities.
• Coached troop softball team, summer of 2004.

Group Leader, 4-H Sheep Division, 2003–2004
• Worked with group of six fifth and sixth grade students to raise Hampshire sheep.
• Sponsored sheep at state fair in Springfield.

References

Available on request.

〉 Yuki Jung

17327 N.E. Waterton
Los Angeles, CA 90069
Yuki.Jung@xxx.com
(213) 555-2239

〉 Job Desired

An internship with the Department of Agriculture as a writer for the
Social Sciences Institute.

〉 Education

University of California, Los Angeles, CA
September 2004–present
Pursuing a double major of English and Environmental Science
Courses of study:
- Writing and Composition
- Advanced courses in copy editing
- Biology
- Microbiology
- Chemistry
- Computer Science

Cathedral High School, 74 Union Park Street, Boston, MA
September 2000–June 2004
Courses taken:
- Typing II
- Marketing and Public Relations
- Computer Applications
- Japanese IV
- Advanced writing courses

〉 Work Experience

Typist at Opti-Craft Laboratory, Inc., Los Angeles, CA
September 2004–present

Secretarial Assistant at Barker Enterprises, Inc., Boston, MA
Summers, 2001, 2002, and 2003

Attendant at Bruce & Bill's Arco Station, Boston, MA
Summer, 2000

❯ Skills

- Type 55 wpm
- Fluent in Japanese
- Familiar with all apects of PageMaker
- Knowledge of *The Chicago Manual of Style* and *The Associated Press Stylebook*
- Digital Photography and Photoshop

❯ Activities

- Future Business Leaders of America
- National Honor Society
- Volleyball
- Yearbook, four years

❯ References

Available on request.

JANINE HARTLEY

168 N.E. Clarkston Street
Battle Creek, MI 49017
Cellular: (616) 555-3420
E-mail: JHartley@xxx.com

JOB SOUGHT

Position in retail sales for hardware or electronic products.

EDUCATION

Battle Creek Central High School, 2000–2004
Battle Creek, MI
Specialized coursework: Computers, Marketing I, Spanish IV,
Accounting II, Electronics, and Woodworking Shop.

EXPERIENCE

Battle Creek Auto Parts, 2002–present
Duties: serve customers, maintain warehouse supply,
stock and shelf parts, receive shipments.

Wendy's Store #1023, 2001–2002
Duties: prepare fast food, process orders, clean-up,
and operate kitchen machinery.

ACTIVITIES

• Spanish Club
• Outdoor school counselor
• JV basketball

REFERENCES

Available on request.

JUAN AGUILAR

158 Halladay S.W.
Benton Harbor, MI 49028
Juan.Aguilar@xxx.com
(616) 555-7379

JOB DESIRED

Printer's apprentice in newspaper printing department.

EDUCATION

Eagle Crest High School, 2001–2005
Pertinent courses: graphic arts, journalism, photography, computer science

SKILLS

Ability to operate the following:
- Graphic printing press
- Screen printer
- Digital camera
- Compugraphic 2824 typesetter
- Macintosh computer (QuarkXPress, PageMaker, Adobe Photoshop)

WORK EXPERIENCE

Production chief for *Eagle Crest Herald* student newspaper
2003–present
- Set up and lay out boards for printing preparation.
- Successfully completed transfer from traditional typesetting and layout to electronic prepress with ability to scan photographs into system, then crop and size electronically to fit layout of text and other graphics.

Printing assistant for Michigan Printing
Summer 2004
- Assisted with preparing camera-ready mechanicals for film, making photo negatives for printing plates, positioning plates on press, checking press runs, operating cutter and folder.
- Worked with stripping department on cutting masks and windows in film.

House painting for private residence, interior and exterior
Summers of 2002 and 2003
- Worked with a crew of eight
- Helped assist with color selection and paint types

REFERENCES

Available on request

◆ Shari Hasak

3320 Delaware Avenue • Erie, NY 14222
Shari.Hasak@xxx.com • (716) 555-2193

◆ Education

2002–present
Marshfield Girls Academy
24 Shoshone Street, Erie, NY

1993–present
Private voice lessons
Roseanne Valdivieso and Pauline Jenson

1992–1998
Ballet lessons
Judy Andresch School of Dance

◆ Experience

Singing Hostess 2003–present
Rheinlander Restaurant, Academy Boulevard, Erie, NY
• Greet and seat customers, and provide musical entertainment.

Delivery Person 2003–present
Balloons, Etc., West McKinley Parkway, Erie, NY
• Drive company van and deliver balloon bouquets, flowers, and singing
  telegrams.

Provide childcare 2000–present
Private homes, Erie, NY
• Care for children ages 2 to 7, provide meals, and perform first aid.

Singer 1997–present
Private weddings and private parties, Erie, NY

◆ Achievements

• Captain, Marshfield Dance Team, 2002–present
• First soloist for the Erie County Youth Choir
• Marshfield Girls' Choir, 2002 and 2003
• Junior Class President, 2003
• Youth of the Month, Erie Elks Lodge No. 125, January 2004
• National Honor Society Scholar of the Year, 2004
• State Letter in girls' volleyball
• Speak conversational German

◆ References

Available upon request.

Latisha Ann Smith

317 W. Trinity, Apt. 6 ▪ Durham, NC 87441
L.Smith@xxx.com ▪ (704) 555-2930

Education

Hillside High School
1900 Concord Street, Durham, NC
Graduated: 2005

Durham Technical Community College
Special Summer Session, Pre-engineering
Summer 2004

Relevant Courses and Training

- Three years of math (including Trigonometry)
- Practical Physics
- Chemistry
- Wood Shop II
- Metals II
- Building Construction
- AutoCAD
- Four years of Mac and PC experience

Experience and Skills

- Assisted with framing and roofing two new houses.
- Completed roof repair project on cedar-shake roof.
- Removed and replaced siding on one wall of shingle-sided house.
- Provided landscape maintenance for private homes, including lawn mowing, weeding, trimming, hedging, and some planting.
- Through school coursework I have developed the ability to operate a lathe, table saw, drill press, and other metal and woodworking machinery.

Work Record

John Jalletty Construction, 421 Driver Street, Durham, NC
June–August 2003

Hillside High School, Wood Shop Assistant, Durham, NC
September 2003–June 2004

References

Available on request.

GARY LUPAS

809 N. Washington Street

Bismarck, ND 58501

Cellular: (974) 555-3994

E-mail: Gary.Lupas@xxx.com

OBJECTIVE

Position in agribusiness utilizing my supervisory and organizational skills.

EDUCATION

Central Senior High School
1000 East Century Avenue, Bismarck, ND
Graduated: 2005
Courses completed: business series courses in agriculture, law, and marketing; special project course in which I devised and prepared a marketing and development plan for a new agricultural support services business.

RELEVANT EXPERIENCE

Hay Bailer/Field Boss, Klair & Klock Larson Farm
Summers 2001–2003
- Worked each summer in berry fields, earning in the top 10 percent of all field hands (paid by ton bailed).
- In 2003, hired as a field boss and supervised workers, paid fees, and checked for quality.

Swim Instructor/Life Guard, Bismarck Community Pool
September 2002–June 2003
- Supervised swim activities at indoor pool facility.
- Taught swimming lessons to 4th, 5th, and 6th grade children.
- Hold current life-saving certificate.

SKILLS & ACTIVITIES

- Experienced with wide range of farm implements and machinery.
- Valid driver's license.
- Swim team member (first place in state competition).
- Member of 4-H Club, 12 years.

References available upon request.

ERIN R. DURANT

223 Brittain Road • Redmond, Washington 98052

E.Durant@xxx.com • (206) 555-3380

EDUCATION

Redmond Senior High School
Expected graduation date: 2006
Dean's List, 8 semesters

Specialized Courses: Home Building Construction, PGE Good Sense Home, Wood Shop, Auto Technology. (4.0 GPA in specialized courses.)

SKILLS

As a result of both regular and freelance employment, I have gained specific job-related skills in the following areas: logging, wood cutting, pipe laying, heavy equipment operation, carpentry, general home maintenance, yard work, house painting, and automotive repair.

WORK EXPERIENCE

Laborer, Jenson Building Management, September 2004
- Stripped and replumbed a bathroom, cleaned gutters, installed insulation, and removed shrubbery.

Laborer, Scott Farris (Private Contractor), Summers 2003 and 2004
- Completed deck repairs, washed and painted buildings, trimmed trees, shored up a retaining wall.
- Assisted with roof repair, window cleaning, car repair, moving, and transportation.

Laborer, Wolcott Excavating, Summers 2001 and 2002
- Worked on ditch digging, ran errands in company truck to obtain pipe and blueprints; made deliveries of pipe and fixtures; read blueprints; installed insulation; took inventory; filled orders; and organized stock.
- Operated chain saw, jumping jack, 580K backhoe, Halton cat loader, Halton cat D4, and Case 24-ton roller; drove dump truck.

I have also worked on several other short-term contractor jobs doing carpentry and general labor.

ACTIVITIES

- Four years on wrestling team; letterman
- Two years on football team
- Track official for the track teams
- Student government
- Building construction and wood shop

References are available upon request

STEPHANIE SABATINI
889 Copley Road
Akron, OH 44308
S.Sabatini@xxx.com
(216) 555-1941

OBJECTIVE
I am seeking a position as a caregiver in a quality preschool or day care environment while I pursue my degree in Education and Early Childhood Development.

EDUCATION
Central Hower High School, 123 N. Forge Street, Akron, OH
Graduated: 2004
Specialized courses: Child Development and Early Childhood Education

Mt. Union College, 1972 Clark Avenue, Akron, OH
Summer of 2003, open enrollment program
Courses: Child Development and Introduction to Psychology

RELATED EXPERIENCE
CHILDCARE: I have been providing competent childcare since 1998. I provide care consistently for four children in two different families.

COUNSELING: In October 2001 and April 2002, I worked as a counselor at the Trout Creek Outdoor School, supervising sixth grade students and teaching basic plant identification and plant ecology. Also presented lessons on plants at several grade schools.

VOLUNTEER: Since June 2001, I have conducted tours at the Akron Park Zoo, educating children about zoo animals, natural habitat, and endangered species. During October 2002 I participated in the "Zoo Boo" Train and dressed in costume and entertained train riders along the route.

REFERENCES
Available on request.

Aisha Mgazi

289 Windfall Drive • Pittsburgh, PA 15236 • A.Mgazi@xxx.com • (412) 555-9027

Job Desired
Sales clerk or customer service representative for major department store.

Education
Baldwin High School
4653 Clairton Boulevard, Pittsburgh, PA
Graduated: 2005

Work Experience
Courtesy Clerk, A&G Food Centers, April 2002–present
Primary responsibilities include assisting customers in locating items and taking purchases to their cars, bag groceries, count bottles, stock shelves, and provide additional assistance as needed.

Assistant, Monograms Plus, Summer 2002 and Christmas Season 2002
Monogrammed shirts, sweatshirts, shorts, and jackets. Also provided customer service and stocked shelves.

Sales Representative, Accents, November 2000 to January 2001
Served customers, coordinated sales, operated the cash register, and assisted with maintaining stock.

Skills
• Accurately operate a cash register and handle cash and credit card financial transfers.
• Strong computer background including Microsoft Word, PageMaker, and Power-Point.
• Fluent in Sign Language.

Activities
• Served as a counselor at a camp specializing in Hearing Impaired children.
• Member of the International Club and Multicultural Students Organization.
• Played three years of volleyball.

References
Available upon request.

BRIAN SCHLOSSER

243 Pleasant Avenue
Providence, RI 02903
Home: (401) 555-6827
Cellular: (401) 555-2335
brianschlosser@xxx.com

OBJECTIVE

To obtain part-time employment as a stage hand in a small theatrical company.

EDUCATION

Hope High School
Graduated: June 2005
GPA: 3.3

Shea High School
Pawtucket, RI
Attended: 2002–2003

RELEVANT EXPERIENCE

- Worked as stage manager for three school productions.
- Operated lights and sound for musical production of *Oklahoma*.
- Assisted with set design and building for three plays.
- Experienced with all aspects of theatrical production.
- Worked as stage hand for a production at Brown University.
- Played the lead in *Brigadoon*.
- Sang in the chorus in *Godspell*.

WORK HISTORY

Cashier and line cook, Taco Time, April 2001–present.

Paper distributor, *Pawtucket Evening News*, March 2001–May 2003.

ACTIVITIES

- Member of Thespian Society.
- Participated in various aspects of student theatrical productions at Hope High School.
- Sang in Madrigal Singers and Concert Choir, Shea High School.

REFERENCES

Available on request.

• LEVAR JOHNSON •

2230 Cunningham Lane
Clarksville, TN 37042
L.Johnson@xxx.com
(615) 555-8117

• JOB SOUGHT

Entry-level technician position

• EDUCATION

Northwest High School
Lafayette Road, Clarksville, TN
Graduated 2004
GPA: 3.87
Major: Technology and Electronics

Civil Air Patrol (U.S. Air Force Auxiliary)
2001 to present

• SKILLS

- Trained in electronics repair at Civil Air Patrol (oscilloscopes, radios, radar)
- Completed two years in technology and electronics courses at Northwest High School
- Repaired disassembled television set to working order
- Experienced in operating compression tools for construction

• WORK HISTORY

Construction Worker, Johnson Construction, April 2000 to present
Major duties: Framed and roofed homes, hauled lumber to job site in company truck, checked lumber delivery against purchase order

Pizza Chef, Little Caesar's, 1998 to 2000

References available upon request

BRIAN VASQUEZ

990 Woody Road, Apt. 15
Dallas, TX 75253
B.Vasquez@xxx.com
(214) 555-2369

OBJECTIVE

A career in business management. Immediate goal is an entry-level position with a growing business.

EDUCATION

Highlands Senior High School
Graduated: May 2004

Specialized Courses:
• Business I & II
• Advanced Computer Science (two years)
• Spanish I & II

EXPERIENCE

Assistant Manager, Taco Bell Restaurant, May 2002 to present
• Started as line cook, June 2002
• Promoted to cashier, November 2002
• Promoted to manager with supervisory responsibility, May 2003

Assistant Manager, Student Store, Highlands Senior High,
September 2001 to June 2002
• Scheduled workers for student store operation
• Checked accuracy of cash reports and tracked any discrepancies
• Assisted manager with ordering stock and receiving shipments

Student Assistant, Counseling Office, Highlands Senior High,
September 2000 to June 2001
• Worked for four counselors, answered telephones, scheduled appoint-
  ments, typed letters
• Student assistants selected on basis of ability, skills, and trustworthiness

Page 1 of 2

ACTIVITIES
- Future Business Leaders of America DECA (Diversified Education Clubs of America, a marketing club)
- Attended Texas Business Week at American Institute of Commerce, Dallas, TX
- Currently Vice President of DECA, which operates the student store at Highlands Senior High School

REFERENCES
Available on request

TAMMY PRYDE

2339 S.E. Kibling Avenue • Tyler, TX 75710

T.Pryde@xxx.com • (214) 555-0422

JOB SOUGHT

Summer internship in graphic design that will utilize my computer drawing and layout skills and provide opportunities for further training.

EDUCATION

Lee High School, Tyler, TX
Graduated: 2005
GPA: 3.29

* Art and Graphics (three years)
* Computer Applications and Programming
* Drafting/Mechanical Drawing
* Web Construction and Design

WORK EXPERIENCE

Graphic Artist, student publications (newspapers, yearbook).

* Designed logos and mastheads.
* Established design formats for entire newspaper.
* Worked with design and production team to design yearbook and cover.
* Set up computer templates on Mac and PC computers.
* Worked with editors on layout of each issue of the newspaper.
* Designed advertisements for student clubs for both publications.
* Created new computer clip art and altered existing art.
* Familiar with Quark, PageMaker, Photoshop, and numerous website management programs.
* Digital photography experience.
* Knowledge of *The Chicago Manual of Style* and *The Associated Press Stylebook*.

References are available on request.

Sherry Gonzalez
235 Gramercy Avenue
Ogden, Utah 84404
(801) 555-1409
s.gonzalez@xxx.com

Objective
Obtain a summer internship with a local business so that I may utilize my clerical skills and learn more about personnel issues. My long-term goal is a career in personnel management.

Education
Ogden Community College, Ogden, Utah
September 2004–present
Currently taking classes in Human Resources and Business Management.

Lamond High School, Ogden, Utah
Graduated: 2004
Served as a counseling office assistant answering telephones, typing documents, filing and scheduling appointments.

Work Experience
Wimpy's Burgers, part-time, 2002 to present
Serve customers, prepare food, operate cash register, handle money, and handle all aspects of closing.

Jazzercise, part-time, 2002 to present
Provide quality care for children of parents participating in Jazzercise exercise programs.

Skills
• Familiar with Macintosh and IBM computers
• Ability to develop, customize, and maintain databases with programs such as ACT! and People Soft
• Type 70 wpm
• Strong telephone communications skills
• Customer service background
• Fluent in conversational Spanish

References available on request

HANNAH WEST

1137 Grove Street • Holland, MI 49423
H.West@xxx.com • (616) 555-2740

OBJECTIVE

Seasonal position as a student teacher for summer art camp programs.

EDUCATION

Timpview High School; Graduated: 2005
Courses include: childhood education, art (two years), advanced studio
painting, and computer applications in art.

EXPERIENCE

• Since June of 1999, I have worked as a child care provider to children of
various ages, responsible for preparing food, feeding, diapering, and
general care.
• Each summer I have worked full-time and offered innovative children's
art projects that were designed for specific ages and abilities.
• In June of 2001 and 2002 I taught art during a vacation Bible school
program for elementary school children.

SPECIAL SKILLS

• Ability to operate a variety of computer software and hardware programs, specifically programs providing graphic arts and page layout
capabilities.
• Hold valid CPR certification.

References and portfolio of children's projects are available on request.

jennifer sungentuck

1589 North Church Street
Rutland, VT 05701
Jenny.Sung@xxx.com
(802) 555-1939

job sought

To obtain a department store security staff position, working evenings or weekends, so I can pursue my education to become a Police Officer.

education

Rutland High School
Class of 2005
GPA: 3.7

State Police Explorer Program
Summer 2001

accomplishments

- Started RADD, Rutlanders Against Drugs and Drinking
- Elected Vice-President of Junior Class, Rutland High School
- Lettered in track and field, volleyball, and softball
- Honor Roll every semester since Freshman year
- Fluent in Japanese

work history

Waitress, The Pines Restaurant, October 2002–present
Duties: greet and serve customers, communicate orders to kitchen staff, direct preparation of salads and desserts. Responsible for quality of service provided to customers. Earned bonus for excellence and courtesy, December 2002.

References are available on request.

Vin Phong

2005 N. Leavitt, Apt. 2
Chicago, IL 60625
Vin.Phong@xxx.com
(773) 555-4958

Objective

Entry-level graphic arts or production position.

Experience

Garfield News Production
Chief, 2003–2004
Graphic Artist, 2002–2003

- Created layout for student newspaper.
- Designed advertisements.
- Prepared paste-up boards for printing.
- Sized and cropped photographs for reproduction.
- Specified type sizes and styles for typesetters.
- Selected and designed art images to enhance visual design of newspaper.
- Worked with editorial staff to determine placement of news articles and photographs.

Freelance Artist, 2004–present

- Designed and prepared mechanicals for logo for my father's restaurant supply business.
- Worked for several student groups to design banners, signs, and logos for school-related activities.

Education

Garfield High School
Graduated: 2005

My elective coursework has focused on art and design, often involving extracurricular projects because I had completed the class assignments and sought additional opportunities to challenge my skills.

References available.

JASON RAINTREE

2268-A South 187th Street
Seattle, WA 98055
(206) 555-9225

OBJECTIVE

Summer internship with social service agency.

EDUCATION

John Glenn High School
4224 South 188th Street, Seattle, WA
Class of 2004
GPA: 3.47

Course work designed to provide broad background with some specific training in areas useful to social services, including:

- Child Development
- Sociology
- Psychology
- Writing for Business
- U.S. Government
- Spanish (three years)

EXPERIENCE & ACHIEVEMENTS

- Volunteer assistant at Boys and Girls Club of South Seattle.
- Coached and refereed elementary school children on sports teams, including basketball, soccer, and softball.
- Helped counselors with "Just Say No" educational programs. Coordinated, with three other students, an anti-drug club that sponsored alcohol and drug-free events and activities as well as an annual drug awareness assembly. In the first year, we had 50 percent participation throughout the school.
- Selected by South Seattle Rotary Club International to present an essay celebrating Seattle's Native American heritage and proposing some remedies for the problems facing Native Americans in today's society.

References available on request

ROBERT GOLDSTEIN

2250 Collins Avenue

Huntington, West Virginia 25702

Bob.Goldstein@xxx.com

(304) 555-9941

JOB SOUGHT
Training position with Huntington Fire District.

EDUCATION
Cabel County Vocational-Technical High School, Class of 2005.
Major: Health and Physical Education.
Courses: health and human fitness, human anatomy, human development, safety and first aid.

EXPERIENCE
Referee, West Hills Soccer Club, 2000–present.
• Work summers and weekends as a referee for soccer games and tournaments for elementary- and junior high school-level soccer teams.

Referee and Ticket Sales, CCVTSHS, 2000–2002.
• Served as practice referee during basketball team practice sessions.
• Sold tickets at entrance for some basketball games.

ACTIVITIES & AWARDS
• President's Council on Physical Fitness.
• Varsity football, letter award.
• Varsity track and field, letter award.

REFERENCES
Available on request.

Anjala Hindagolla

2325 Rapids Drive
Racine, Wisconsin 53406
(414) 555-8733

Objective

Cook or chef's assistant position in Middle Eastern restaurant. Currently pursuing an Associates in Culinary Arts at night.

Experience

Ramdalla Cafe, Milwaukee, WI, 2003–2004
   • *Worked in family restaurant as chef's assistant.*
   • *Operated kitchen machinery including mixers and slicer.*
   • *Prepared foods from recipes.*
   • *Maintained oven and grill cleanliness.*
   • *Prepared serving plates for beautiful visual presentation.*
   • *Gained experience in all aspects of restaurant food preparation.*

Education

Case High School, Racine, WI
Class of 2002
Specialized courses:
   • *Home Economics I and II*
   • *Food Science and Nutrition*
   • *Business Operations*
   • *Food Preparation and Safety (special workshop at state health division)*

References

Available on request.

Ramon Lopez

356 N. Alameda
Santa Rosa, CA 95406
(707) 555-3964

Objective

Summer carpenter crew position with home construction company.

Experience

Tiara Construction Company, Carpentry
5316 S.E. Francis St., Sebastapol, CA
Summers 2003 and 2004
Supervisor: George Linde, (707) 555-5015
• Worked with carpentry crew; framed and roofed houses;
sheet rocked interiors; and installed insulation in walls.

Growers Outlet, Stocker
15165 S.E. Laguna Blvd., Santa Rosa, CA
September 2003 to present
Supervisor: Janet Brendler, (707) 555-2000
• Work with grocery supervisor to stock shelves, receive and direct shipments
of produce, and maintain quality presentation in produce department.

Education

Santa Rosa High School
2156 Cerritos, Santa Rosa, CA
Graduated: 2005
Pertinent courses: Wood Shop, Metal Shop, Building Construction,
Mechanical Drawing, and Architecture.

References

Available on request.

LYNN SIMMONS

2620 Harrison Avenue
Cheyenne, WY 82001
(307) 555-2883

JOB SOUGHT

Summer firefighting crew position with the U.S. Forest Service.

EDUCATION

Central Senior High School
5500 Education Drive, Cheyenne, WY
Graduated: June 2005

TRAINING

- Valid CPR/Lifesaving Certificate.
- Trained in firefighting and prevention by Cheyenne County Fire Department.

EXPERIENCE

U.S. Forest Service, Summer 2004

Spent two weeks with fire crew in Yellowstone National Park on fire damage control. Dug fire trenches, cleared brush, and opened clogged stream beds.

U.S. Forest Service, Summer 2003

Worked as camp cook's assistant on fire crew on site in Yellowstone National Park. Maintained food provisions for firefighters, assisted with first aid treatment of minor burns, served meals, worked at camp canteen.

REFERENCES

Available at your request.

Janice Anne Richland

10205 Catlin Avenue • Brookline, MA 02146
Home: (617) 555-0116 • Cell: (617) 555-7567

Objective
Retail music store sales position.

Skills
- Good knowledge of both contemporary and classical music.
- Work well with others and a very quick learner.
- Able to operate cash registers and most office equipment.

Work Experience
Cashier, A&W Rootbeer Stand, June 2004–present
Supervisor: Raejean Matthews, (617) 555-9444
Duties: Greet customers, take orders, communicate orders to line cooks, operate
        cash register, handle cash, close and balance register receipts at shift's
        end.

Clerical Assistant, Brookline High School, Summer 2003
Supervisor: Annette Jameson, (617) 555-7800
Duties: Answered telephones, routed calls through six-line switchboard, typed
        letters, filed, greeted visitors, assisted teachers and students as
        needed.

Education
Brookline High School, Brookline, MA
Graduated: June 2005
Pertinent Courses: Wind ensemble, orchestra, jazz band, choir, music theory,
        business.

Standish Middle School, Boston, MA
September 2001–June 2002
Pertinent Courses: Concert Band, Jazz Band.

Achievements
- First place league solo, 2003
- Four Outstanding Solo Jazz awards, 2002–2003
- MAME Youth Series O.S.O., 2002
- All-State Band, 2003
- Honor Roll student

References Available

MASOUD YASMIR ◆ ◆ ◆

211 South Grevillea Avenue, Apt. 26B
Inglewood, CA 90301
M.Yasmir@xxx.com
(213) 555-9562

◆ OBJECTIVE

To obtain an entry-level position in electronics design and manufacturing.

◆ EDUCATION

Morningside High School, Class of 2005
GPA: 3.9

Pertinent Courses:
- Electronics
- Computer Applications
- Algebra I and II
- Trigonometry
- Precalculus

◆ EXPERIENCE

Assistant to Electronics Teacher, Morningside High School, 2003–present
- Completed all available course work in electronics.
- Functioned as lab instructor during beginning electronics courses.

◆ ACHIEVEMENTS

- Developed radar device for activating electronic control panel.
- Coordinated project for lighting student theater.
- Built and operated control board for sound and light productions.
- Built and customized computer hard disk drive for personal computer.
- Experienced in repair of stereos, video cassette recorders, DVD and CD players.
- Taking computer classes at City College.

◆ REFERENCES

Available on request.

John Umiak

P.O. Box 1648
Palmer, Alaska 99645
J.Umiak@xxx.com
(907) 555-8406

Objective

Career in fisheries and wildlife.

Education

Sustina Valley Junior–Senior High School
Graduated: 2004.
GPA 3.6.
• Courses were primarily in biological sciences, with an emphasis in special projects on salmonid fishes.

Matanuska-Sustina College, 2004–present
• Currently taking courses in computers, general biology, chemistry, and marine biology.

Experience

Matanuska Fisheries, June 2004–present
Work on fishing boat crew, fishing for salmon, halibut, and crab. Maintain fishing equipment, check fishing nets daily for damage, and repair them as needed.

Independent project, 2002–2003
Coordinated research project on salmon runs in local stream. Working with my high school biology teacher, I designed research procedures, collected data, and discovered a 20 percent decrease in salmon populations between the 1997 and 1998 spring Chinook runs.

References available on request.

A M A N D A   M A R T I N

1076 North 27th Street
Phoenix, AZ 85028
Mandy.Martin@xxx.com
(602) 555-3874

G O A L

A career in the computer industry as a programmer.

E D U C A T I O N

Shadow Mountain High School, 2003–2005
GPA: 3.75

Relevant Courses:
- Computer Science
- Computer Applications
- Computer Programming
- Algebra
- Geometry
- Trigonometry
- Precalculus

A C H I E V E M E N T S

- Worked on five-member team to develop new computer software for grading multiple-choice tests, recording grades, and providing bell curves and other averages that could be used for assigning letter grades.
- Customized programming software for use by students with visual impairments.
- Won annual district prize for best computer programming solution.

R E F E R E N C E S

Available upon request.

Christina Wu

3826 Sweetwater Avenue
Cincinnati, OH 20999
Christy.Wu@xxx.com
(601) 555-2834

Objective

Summer internship with law office.

Education

Chaparral High School, Class of 2005
Academic standing: 20th in class of 420
GPA: 4.0

Courses taken:
Business Law, Business Practices, Computer Applications
(word processing, spreadsheets, and databases), Journalism, Career Options: Law

Achievements

- BPOE Elks Scholarship
- Zimmerman Scholarship
- Student of the Month, Cincinnati Elks Club
- President, National Honor Society
- Student Senator, Sophomore and Junior years
- Chaparral High Scholarship and Leadership Award
- Dean's List

Memberships

- Chaparral Thespians
- Cincinnati First Methodist Church
- Youth Choir
- Chaps (high school jazz ensemble)

References available on request.

Jerome Washington

3705 Hunnington Street
Little Rock, AK 54662
J.Washington@xxx.com
Cell: (501) 555-3785

Objective

A career in computer programming and development

Education

McClellan High School
Graduated: 2005
GPA: 3.98

Relevant Courses

- Computer Programming (BASIC, PASCAL, DOS, C++, COBAL, Cold Fusion, PHP)
- Computer Applications (Microsoft Word, PowerPoint, Photoshop, Quark, Access, dBase, Symphony, Apache)
- Electronics (including microchip technology)
- Four years of math

Honors

- McClellan Senior Scholarship
- Little Rock Masonic Scholarship
- Most Innovative Computer Solution Award, *cBasic Magazine*
- Elected Treasurer, Computer J's Club

Work History

Computer Programmer, Internship, Huber Reality, Summer 2004
Waiter, Genrette's Ice Cream Parlor, 2003–present
Station Attendant, Scott's Chevron, 2002–2003

References Available

SHAWANA HARRIS

110 Royal Scots Way, Apt. 245

Bakersfield, CA 93306

Home: (805) 555-3746

Cell: (805) 555-8892

OBJECTIVE
Customer service job with computer company.

EDUCATION
Foothill High School, 501 Park Drive, Bakersfield, CA
Graduated: 2005
GPA: 3.2

Special courses:
- ◆ Advanced Computer Applications (Adobe Creative Suite, Microsoft Office Suite, Macromedia Studio MX)
- ◆ Business Applications
- ◆ Accounting

Special activities:
- ◆ Served as clerical assistant for English teachers.
- ◆ Worked as a clerk in the student store.
- ◆ Planned and carried out activities as part of the Homecoming and Senior Prom committees.
- ◆ Played varsity basketball (top scorer last season).
- ◆ Made the honor roll four out of six semesters.

EXPERIENCE
Student Assistant, FHS Computer Lab, 2003–2004.
- ◆ Worked with computer teacher.
- ◆ Installed and initialized software on lab computers.
- ◆ Maintained student use records for lab.
- ◆ Assisted students with questions about computer software.
- ◆ Supervised checkout of lab materials.
- ◆ Helped update new hardware for the entire computer lab.

References available on request

SHARONE DAVIS

22200 Division Street, Apt. 315 • Los Angeles, CA 93535
(805) 555-3736 • sharonedavis@xxx.com

OBJECTIVE

Entry-level position with production department of newspaper or printing firm.

EDUCATION

Antelope Valley High School, Class of 2004
GPA: 3.48

Pertinent courses: Photography, Darkroom Techniques, Graphic Design, Introduction to Art, Mechanical Drawing.

EXPERIENCE

Darkroom Technician, Antelope High School, *Viewpoint* (student newspaper), 2003–2004

Duties: developed, proofed, and printed black-and-white film; prepared PMTs of line art in specified enlargements and reductions; made halftoned prints for direct paste-up; made negatives to size for stripping into plate-ready film.

Layout Artist, Antelope High School, *Viewpoint*, 2002–2003

Duties: Responsible for computerized layout of paper using Macintosh computer and QuarkXPress layout software. Gathered materials for publication and ensured accuracy and integrity of design throughout.

REFERENCES

Available on request.

Michael Han

435 South Monaco Parkway
Denver, Colorado 80204
(303) 555-4481
michaelhan@xxx.com

Education

West High School, 951 Elati Street, Denver, Colorado 2000–2004.
GPA: 3.86.

Aachen Gymnasium, Bonn, West Germany, 2002–2003 (Exchange Student).

Skills & Achievement

- Trained in basic bookkeeping, invoicing, inventory, and payroll procedures.
- Speak fluent Chinese and German; working knowledge of French.
- Experienced with various computer software and hardware, including MS DOS, Macintosh, and Linux operating platforms; WordPerfect, Microsoft Word, and MacWrite word processing; Lotus and Works spreadsheets; and dBase and Filemaker Oracle software, among others.
- Provided customer service in small retail sales outlet for computer equipment.
- Excellent writing and communications skills.
- Effective leadership skills; served as president of senior class, vice-president of junior class, student senator during first and second years.
- Selected by American Field Service (AFS) as exchange student to Aachen, West Germany.

Employment History

Summer Sales Intern, Computer Express, Denver, Colorado, Summers 2002–2004.

Duties: Provided information and assistance to clients in small computer hardware and software dealership that handled both IBM and compatibles and Macintosh computers. Self-trained in a wide range of software in order to better match appropriate software and hardware systems to clients' needs.

REFERENCES AVAILABLE

Mark Bettorini

2100 West Oxford Avenue
Englewood, CO 80110
(303) 555-3422
markbettorini@xxx.com

Objective

Career in forestry/wood products industry that will utilize my science background, timber experience, and leadership skills.

Experience

Fire Watch/Tree Planter, U.S. Forest Service, Denver. Summer 2003.

Crew Leader, Colorado Highway Department, Grounds Crew. Summer 2002.

Twelve years as a Boy Scout with woodsman badges and outdoor survival training.

Education

- Sheridan High School, Englewood, Class of 2004; major: Science Leadership.
- Student Body Vice-President, Sheridan High School, 2002–2003.
- President, Sheridan Hikers Club, 2001–2002.
- President, American Junior Red Cross, 2003.
- Vice-President, Science Club, 2001–2003.
- Captain, Sheridan High School Archery Team, 2000–2003.
- Founding Member, Sheridan High Key Club (volunteer service agency), 2000.
- Honors Junior Science Student of the Year, 2003.
- Rotary Club International Exchange Student to New Zealand, spring 2002.
- Key Club Volunteer of the Month, December 2002.

References are available on request.

JUDY REIMER

128 Orange Street • New Haven, CT 06510
(203) 555-3754 • judyreimer@xxx.com

OBJECTIVE

To secure a position as a paralegal in which my education and writing and research skills can be utilized to enhance the effectiveness of a small- to medium-sized law firm.

EDUCATION

Hillhouse High School, 480 Sherman Parkway, New Haven, CT; diploma awarded May 2004.

Concentration: Business, Accounting I and II, Computer Applications (word processing, spreadsheet, database, and communications software for Windows operating platforms), Business Operations (clerical systems).

GPA: 3.75.

EXPERIENCE

Office Assistant. Switter, Harvey, Jenkins & Hewitt, Attorneys at Law, 2002–present.
Duties: Assist attorneys and legal secretaries. Type and proof legal forms. Answer telephone calls on ten-line switchboard. Organize office law library and reshelve books.

Student Assistant. Hillhouse High School, Attendance Office, 2001–2002.
Duties: Assisted staff secretaries with typing, filing, answering telephones, and duplication. Distributed mail to teachers and administrators. Distributed work orders to teachers. Operated stencil machine, photocopier, fax, and six-line switchboard.

ACTIVITIES & ACHIEVEMENTS
Secretary, National Honor Society, 2003–2004
Senior Editor, Sheridan High School Annual, 2003–2004
Team Captain, Sheridan Girls Softball Team, 2003–2004
Copy Editor, *Sheridan High School Annual*, 2002–2003
Member, Future Business Leaders of America, 2000–2002
Member, Thespians (participated in three theatrical productions), 2000-2003

REFERENCES
Available on request

Muhammed Alou

126 S. Granby
Hartford, CT 06112
(203) 555-6623
muhammedalou@xxx.com

EDUCATION: Buckley High School, 300 Wethersfield Avenue, Hartford,
                     CT, Class of 2005

                     Held 4.0 grade point average in all math, business, writ-
                     ing, and English courses.

                     Listed in of *Who's Who Among American High School
                     Students.*

LEADERSHIP: Presided over Business Club. Planned programs, managed
                     budget, set meeting agendas, and organized meetings and
                     club activities, 2003-2004.

                     Elected Secretary of the Student Senate. Responsible for
                     maintaining *Robert's Rules of Order*, 2003-2004.

                     Managed budget, personnel time sheets, and all-school
                     database for student publication. Used Microsoft Office
                     software on Macintosh computers, 2003-2004.

                     Received full scholarship to attend Student Government
                     Conference at State Capitol, summer 2002.

                     Supervised volunteer labor while working at Hartford's
                     Capitol grounds, spring 2002.

EXPERIENCE: Business Manager, *The Hart* (student annual),
                     2001-2004.

                     Groundskeeper, Buckley High School, 2000-2004.

                     Corpsmember, U.S. Federal Government, Youth Conserva-
                     tion Corps, 2000-2002.

REFERENCES AVAILABLE UPON REQUEST

Mary Jo Baptiste
2240 N.W. Nebraska Avenue
Washington, DC 20016
(202) 555-7465
maryjobaptiste@xxx.com

OBJECTIVE
To obtain a training position as a preschool guide in a Montessori preschool.

EDUCATIONAL BACKGROUND
Coolidge High School, Washington, DC, Graduated: 2004.

Relevant Courses: Human Development, Childhood Education, Psychology, Sociology, Social Science, Speech and Communications.

Honors: *Who's Who Among American High School Students*, Future Teachers of America, Volunteer Student Activist of the Year (all-school nomination), District of Columbia Youth of the Month (President's Council on Youth), Quill and Scroll (journalism honor society).

EXPERIENCE
Parks & Recreation Day Camp Leader, Washington, DC,
Summers 2002 and 2003.
Planned programs for children 4–8 years old. Built rapport and communications with parents. Provided supervision of children on play structures during breaks. Taught teamwork skills through problem solving in groups of six children. Taught crafts, songs, and dances. Led storytelling for children aged 10–14.

Outdoor School Counselor and Instructor, DC School District
2001–2003.
Counseled, supervised, and instructed sixth-grade students from various Washington elementary schools during one-week program each spring. Assumed responsibility for twelve girls. Served as live-in counselor three years, one year as instructor emphasizing environmental education.

Other part-time employment: Waitress, housekeeper, clerical assistant.

SPECIAL SKILLS AND INTERESTS
Reporter on the high school newspaper staff for two years. Published an article in the city paper, Washington, DC, February 2004. Knowledge of Native American culture, including traditional songs, dances, and crafts.

References are available upon request.

Craig Kohanek

1851 S. Edwards Road, No. 59
Wilmington, DE 19809
Home: 302-555-7229
Cell: 302-555-1762
craigkohanek@xxx.com

Objective

To obtain a position in sales in an organization oriented toward customer service.

Education

Mount Pleasant High School, Washington Boulevard, Wilmington, DE.
Class of 2005.

Course of study includes:
- Business I and II (organizational structures, economics of business, business ethics, business law, personnel management, business regulations).
- Computer Systems (software applications in word processing, database management, accounting, and communications).
- Office Management (clerical operations, bookkeeping, basic accounting).

Experience

Library Assistant, Mt. Pleasant High School Library, Wilmington.
January 2002-present.
- Organize and record use of magazines in periodicals section. Instruct students on library research techniques and microfilm usage. Answer questions. Maintain copy machine. Reshelve books.

Cashier, Hartford Country Club Golf Shop, Hartford.
June-September 2003.
- Sold rounds of golf, clubs, shoes, and miscellaneous equipment. Monitored driving range. Supervised and participated in cleaning and maintenance of club house.

Retail Sales Clerk, Stan's Shoe Shop, Hartford.
June-September 2001 and 2002.
- Trained in sales and customer service. Greeted customers, took measurements, assisted with style and color selection, ran cash register. Received and accounted for delivered merchandise on corresponding purchase orders and invoices. Designed and set up seasonal displays.

Page 1 of 2

Leadership Experience

Student Tutor, Mt. Pleasant High School, English classes, 2002-2003.
Student Representative, Mt. Pleasant High School Senate, 2002-2003.
Competitor, Mt. Pleasant High School Forensics Squad, 2000-2003.
Representative, Mt. Pleasant High School Model United Nations, 2004.

Extracurricular Activities

Varsity Basketball, 2002-2004.
Varsity Cross Country, 2000-2004.
Concert Choir, First United Church, 1999-present.

REFERENCES AVAILABLE ON REQUEST

Jeanette Bouchardon

21 Lawrence Street N.W. • Washington, DC 20017
(202) 555-2951 • jeanettebouchardon@xxx.com

Objective

To obtain a position in international business in which my bilingual skills and experience in sales and customer service will be used to advantage.

Experience

Holiday Inn Corporation, Washington, DC, 2003 and 2004 (summers)
Assistant Night Manager
• Assisted with translation for French-speaking guests
• Coordinated night-shift activities
• Managed front-desk operations

La Maison Bleu, Washington, DC, 2003–2004 (part-time)
Hostess
• Assisted with translation for French-speaking guests
• Supervised cash register
• Supervised table setting

Nordstrom's Department Store, Washington, DC,
2002–2003 (weekends)
Salesperson
• Sold women's sportswear, cosmetics, and jewelry
• Maintained accurate balance sheets, accounting for all sales
• Recipient of August 2003 Sales Award (based on per-work-hour sales)

Education

Washington International School, 3100 Macomb Street, N.W.,
Washington, DC
• Honors student with GPA: 5.8 (6.0 scale)
• Graduated: May 2005

Special Skills

• Fluent French speaker (child of French parents; mother member of Corps Diplomatique)
• Excellent interpersonal communications skills
• General knowledge of import-export restrictions between U.S. and E.E.C.

References available on request.

sharon flaherty

1250 Harvard Street N.W. • Washington, DC 20009
(202) 555-4119
sharonflaherty@xxx.com

objective

To obtain a position as an assistant librarian in which I can utilize my interpersonal and organizational skills.

education

St. Anselm's Academy, Washington, DC, Class of 2004
Relevant Courses Taken:
- Business
- Office Systems
- Computers in Business (including all MS Office programs)
- Research Strategies
- English/Writing (four years)

experience

Student Librarian, St. Anselm's Academy, October 2002-May 2004
Responsibilities:
- Checked books out to students and teachers.
- Maintained records of books on loan.
- Checked returned books against borrowing records.
- Advised students in the use of the card catalog.
- Assisted users with computer database.
- Answered questions about reference materials.
- Maintained accurate shelving of books and periodicals.

special skills and achievements

- Experienced with on-line database references for library (use *Reader's Guide to Periodical Literature, Business Periodicals Index, Science Periodicals Index*, among others).
- Selected as High School Student of the Month (March 2003) for ongoing volunteer activities with Stone Soup, an urban hunger project.
- Experienced with use of computers for word processing, page layout, and database management (Illustrator, WordPerfect, Photoshop, and Microsoft Works).
- Listed on Honor Roll each year; member of National Honor Society.

References are available at your request.

CLAIRE RENARD

618 N.W. Eighth Street, No. 215

Boca Raton, FL 33486

Telephone: (561) 555-1400

ClaireRenard@xxx.com

OBJECTIVE

To obtain a position that will lead to a career in banking in which my skills in finance, accounting, and organization can be utilized effectively.

EDUCATION

Boca Raton High School, 1501 N.W. Fifteenth Street, Boca Raton, FL
Class of 2004

Pertinent Courses: Business I and II, Economics, Accounting I and II, Business Writing, Office Management Systems, Typing I and II.

ACHIEVEMENTS

Elected Student Body Treasurer. Chaired Finance Committee. Maintained student account books. Recorded income from student fund drives and disbursements for student charities and activities, 2003-2004.

Served on the Finance Committee for the Student Government, 2001-2004.

Coordinated Student Fund Drive, which raised 20 percent more than the previous year's drive to benefit children's programs in Palm Beach County. Served as liaison with local community service center for direction of funds disbursement, 2002-2003.

Acted as Committee Representative to Student Body Executive Board. Attended meetings and presented financial reports to student body officers and advisors, 2002-2003.

ACHIEVEMENTS *(continued)*

Elected President of Business Club. Coordinated monthly meetings. Supervised planning for Business Career Day, 2003-2004.

Served as Treasurer of the Debate Club. Maintained records of dues and expenses for field trips and school visitations, 2001-2002.

Working knowledge of French. Completed four years of high school French and spent one month living in Quebec as part of an intensive language program.

OTHER ACTIVITIES

- Member of National Honor Society
- Girls' Cross Country Track Team
- Social Committee
- Club Français
- Homecoming Committee

References available on request

GRETCHEN MORRISON

2506 Chelsea Street • Tampa, Florida 33603
(813) 555-8220 • gretchenmorrison@xxx.com

OBJECTIVE

Entry-level position that will lead to a career in social service.

EDUCATION

Temple Heights Christian School, Tampa, Florida
Graduated: May 2005

Relevant Coursework: Human Development, Education, Social Science, Public Government, Civics, Speech Communication

EXPERIENCE

Volunteer Coordinator, Project Second Wind, Tampa Central District, 2004
Duties:
• Coordinated volunteers from five Tampa high schools.
• Planned strategies for publicity, volunteer solicitation, site coordination, and area canvassing.
• Plotted maps for canvassing communities.
• Worked with National Guard dispatch office to coordinate drivers for collecting food donations through canvassing.
• On day of drive, supervised canvassing efforts for the five areas. Coordinated delivery to central warehouse.

Volunteer, Meals on Wheels, Tampa, 2004-2005
Duties:
• Prepared individual meal servings for weekly delivery to invalids in Tampa area. Delivered meals and visited with invalids.

Counselor, Summer Camp, Temple Heights Christian School, 2003-2004
Duties:
• Assumed responsibility for twelve girls ages 8-12.
• Prepared and presented lessons in Bible study and environmentalism.
• Provided guitar accompaniment for camp sing-alongs.

ACTIVITIES

- Active member of Say No club, which sponsored drug awareness programs at local elementary schools.
- Worked with student committees to plan social events.
- Helped with publicity for student elections.
- Played on softball team sponsored by local business.

References: Available on request.

Jameson W. Brussard Jr.

212 N. Jefferson Street • Albany, GA 31701
(912) 555-2239 • jamesonbrussard@xxx.com

Objective

A position in customer service leading to a career in business management.

Sales Experience

Served as salesperson in sporting goods store. Over six-month period, made consistent increases in sales, which led to my being selected as salesperson of the quarter, spring 2002.

Sold compact discs and cassettes for a music store. Maintained position among top ten salespeople. Became very knowledgeable about both classical and contemporary music.

Leadership

Elected Senior Class Vice President, 2001–2002. Oversaw committees and served as senior class representative to Student Senate. Assumed responsibilities of class president in her absence.

Revived Business Club; served as president, 2003–2004. Set meeting agendas, presided over meetings, instituted fund drive to sponsor professional visits and field trips, organized trips to local business organizations.

Management

Managed Student Store, Monroe High School, 2002–2004. Supervised student clerks, scheduled work shifts, ordered supplies, received shipments and checked them against purchase orders, served customers.

Serve as Weekend Night Manager at Motel Orleans, a 125-room motel, July 2004–present. Greet guests, manage registration desk, supervise night staff, and serve as security representative on alternating weekends.

Page 1 of 2

Work History

Weekend Night Manager, Motel Orleans, Albany, GA
July 2004–present

Salesperson, Jefferson's Sporting Goods, Albany, GA
May 2003–June 2004

Salesperson, Musicland, Albany, GA
June 2000–May 2003

Education

Monroe High School, Albany, GA
Class of 2004

Activities & Memberships

- Business Club
- Forensics Club
- National Honor Society
- Pep Club
- Publicity Committee
- Photography Club
- JV and Varsity Wrestling

References

Available on request

SAMUEL JUN-LAN CHEN

2110 Cottage Grove Avenue
Chicago Heights, IL 60411
(847) 555-2645
Samuel-Chen@xxx.com

OBJECTIVE

To obtain a laboratory research assistant position in a scientific lab.

EDUCATION

Bloom High School
Chicago Heights, IL
Graduated with highest honors, 2004
GPA: 3.96

RELEVANT COURSES TAKEN
• Biology (two years)
• General Chemistry (one year)
• Organic Chemistry (one year)
• Physics (one year)
• Botany (one semester)
• Math (Algebra, Trigonometry, Calculus)

EXPERIENCE

Laboratory Assistant, Bloom High School, Chemistry Section
2003–2004
• Assisted teacher with laboratory preparation and set-up
• Answered student questions about laboratory experiments
• Graded lab worksheets and recorded grades for chemistry teacher
• Maintained chemical stockroom and kept track of supplies

Laboratory Assistant, Bloom High School, Biology Section
2002–2003
• Assisted with laboratory preparation and clean-up
• Worked with students on dissection projects (frog, fetal pig heart)
• Graded student lab worksheets
• Installed and tested new computer software for simulated dissection
• Directed students in use of computer software

Page 1 of 2

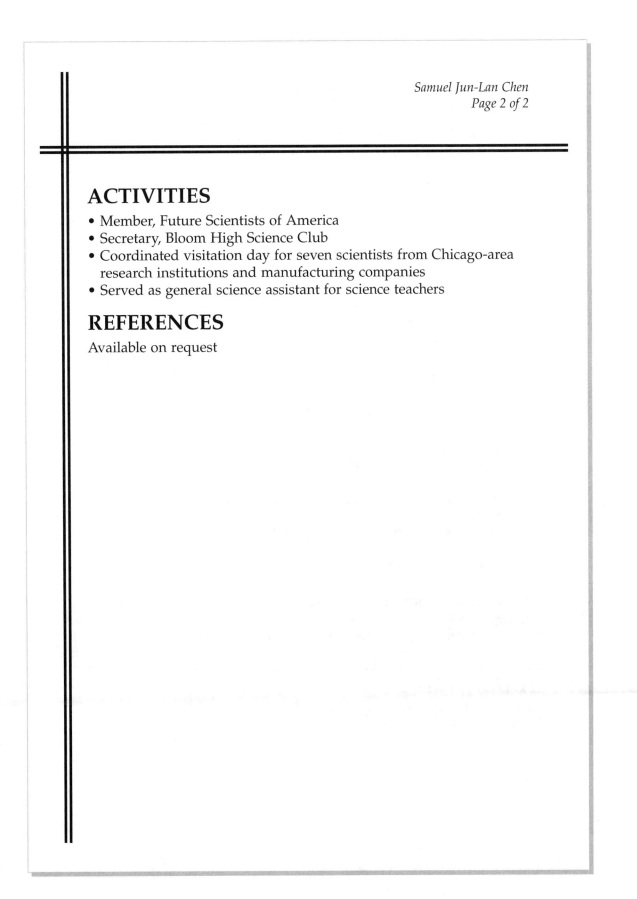

ACTIVITIES

- Member, Future Scientists of America
- Secretary, Bloom High Science Club
- Coordinated visitation day for seven scientists from Chicago-area research institutions and manufacturing companies
- Served as general science assistant for science teachers

REFERENCES

Available on request

STEWART SULLIVAN

1220 North Cole Road • Boise, Idaho 83709
208-555-2477 • stewartsullivan@xxx.com

OBJECTIVE

To secure a position on the production staff of a printing company that will utilize my skills with graphic design and layout.

EXPERIENCE

Graphic Artist, Student Yearbook Staff, 2002–2004

- Assumed responsibility for overall design concepts in 212-page hardbound yearbook.
- Provided design assistance to editorial staff and developed graphic elements for pages needing artwork.
- Designed page layouts using Adobe Illustrator and Quark Xpress.
- Mastered computer page-layout technology and desktop publishing software.
- Prepared photographs for publication (cropped, sized) with Adobe Photoshop.
- Supervised staff of production assistants.

Production Assistant, *Borah Gazette*, 2001–2003

- Prepared layout for student newspaper.
- Cropped, sized, and positioned photographs.
- Designed graphics to accent advertisement section.

EDUCATION

Borah Senior High School, Boise, Idaho
Class of 2004
GPA in art: 4.0

References Available.

PETER PERKINS

601 E. Allis Drive • Milwaukee, WI 53201
(414) 555-1133 • peterperkins@xxx.com

OBJECTIVE

A career in the manufacturing field.

EDUCATION

Milwaukee Vocational High School, Milwaukee, WI
Graduated: 2005

Course Work
• Manufacturing Design (Employing AutoCAD)
• Wood Shop
• Welding
• Drafting
• Technical Writing
• Auto Shop

WORK HISTORY

Wisconsin Manufacturing Company, Milwaukee, WI
Forklift Driver, Summers 2003, 2004
• Drove forklifts
• Repaired and serviced heavy machinery

Penner Furniture, Inc., West Allis, WI
Warehouse Assistant, 2001–2003
• Prepared furniture for delivery
• Organized furniture stock
• Delivered furniture
• Assisted in construction of furniture racks

REFERENCES AVAILABLE

❖ Joanna C. Harper ❖

1150 S. 16th Street
Decatur, IL 62521
(847) 555-2366
joannaharper@xxx.com

❖ Job Sought

Word processing operator, full-time summer employment.

❖ Education and Training

MacArthur High School, Decatur, IL
Graduated: 2005

My major area of emphasis has been business, with course work in office procedures, business machines, business communications, keyboarding (beginning and advanced), computer applications, and accounting.

Specific training includes computer graphics, word processing, data processing, and electronic spreadsheet. I have also received some basic instruction in desktop publishing. My word processing speed is 65 wpm, and I operate a 10-key adding machine at approximately 35 npm.

❖ Work Experience

James Brophy, D.D.S., Summer 2004
1267 S. 15th Street, Decatur, IL
Supervisor: Mrs. Dionne Avery, (847) 555-0112
Job duties: assisted with word processing, filing, typing, answering telephones, scheduling appointments, and managing the reception desk.

Mr. Arva Ellison, 1999–2004
7878 S. Cantrell Street, Decatur, IL
Job duties: provided child care for three children, part-time throughout the school year and full-time during the summer.

❖ Work Experience (continued)

Ellison Farms, 988 Meadow Road, Decatur, IL
Summers 1998 and 1999
Job duties: operated seeder, assisted with harvest of a variety of crops, assisted with irrigation systems, and provided general labor.

❖ Activities

- Varsity Rally Squad: Basketball
- Played flute in Concert Band
- Recreational Cross-Country Ski Club
- Drama Club

❖ References

Available on request

Parker Adams

226 N. Fifth Street, Apt. 42 • Fairbury, Illinois 61739
(815) 555-1154 • parkeradams@xxx.com

Position Desired

Full-time summer employment that makes use of my background as a lab assistant and agricultural worker. My long-term career goal is to become a biomedical engineer.

Education and Training

Prairie Central High School, Fairbury, Illinois
Graduated: 2005

My major area of emphasis has been science. During the past three years, I have completed all of the science courses offered at PCHS, including Biology, Chemistry, Anatomy and Physiology, Physics, Earth Science, Field Biology, Horticulture, and Advanced Chemistry. I have participated in extra-credit research projects in most of these courses. Science GPA: 3.68.

Experience

Organization: As a lab assistant in the science program, I have organized labs, maintained inventory of supplies, entered data into the computer, and assisted students with class assignments.

Equipment: I have operated microscopes, digital meters, and oscilloscopes. I also drive a tractor when working on my grandfather's seed farm.

Efficiency: During my junior year, I worked as a laborer on the family farm approximately 20 hours per week. I was concurrently working on a special honors science project, which required several hours each week of after-school study. I was able to manage my time efficiently and maintain a 3.9 GPA for the year.

Honors

• First Place Project Award, Science VII, Regional Skills Conference, 2004
• Honorable Mention, Science VI, Regional Skills Conference, 2003

References Available

ASSAN MASOUD

228 West Fifth Street, P.O. Box 286
Emporia, KS 66801
(316) 555-2251
assanmasoud@xxx.com

JOB SOUGHT

Full-time summer position with manufacturing company or warehouse.

EDUCATION

Emporia High School, Emporia, KS
Class of 2005

EXPERIENCE

Jayhawk Auto Parts, Emporia, KS
Clerk, Summers 2002 and 2003

Duties: Serve customers, answer questions about auto parts and other merchandise, maintain order in stockroom, find parts by order number on stock shelves, remove items sold from computer inventory, assist with receiving shipments, and enter new stock in computer inventory.

ACTIVITIES

• Varsity and junior varsity sports: football, basketball, baseball, Freshman football, cross country
• Webdesign Club
• Key Club
• Spirit Club

REFERENCES

Available on request

Laura Chen

5527 N.W. Oak Creek Road • Ashland, Oregon 97520
(503) 555-9982 • laurachen@xxx.com

Job Sought: Entry-level position in the field of environmental
                           economics.

Education & Training: **Mt. Ashland Senior High School, Ashland, Oregon**
                           Graduation Class of 2004; GPA: 3.95

                           Courses:
                           • Earth Science
                           • Business Communications
                           • Horticulture
                           • Economics & Government
                           • Biology
                           • Capstone Economics
                           • Algebra 1 & 2
                           • Computer Applications
                           • Probability & Statistics
                           • Computer Keyboarding

Work Experience: **Prudential Bache Securities**, Internship,
                           Summer 2003
                           One Union Square, Suite 2400, Seattle, Washington
                           Supervisor: Kathryn Mix, (205) 555-9111

                           Duties: Posted account records in ledger and con-
                           ducted research on major corporations. Major area
                           of interest was product liability suits against corpora-
                           tions filing Chapter II to escape same suit.

                           Brown's Steak House,
                           October 2002 to present
                           17 First Street, Ashland, Oregon
                           Supervisor: Joseph Brown, (503) 555-2219

                           Duties: Hostess in charge of seating clients at the
                           restaurant during peak evening hours. Manage
                           cashier's station. Work part-time while going to
                           school.

Work Experience:
(Continued)

Oregon River Experience,
Summers 1994 to present
34497 Tall Pines Drive, Grants Pass, Oregon
Supervisor: John Hendersen, (503) 555-2294

Duties: From May to October (with the exception of 2003) I have worked either as a lead guide or a support guide. As a lead guide, I lead raft trips down the Rogue River, organize equipment and travel logistics, plan and cook meals, and am responsible for knowledge of the river and surrounding area as well as for the safety and equipment of a group of 25 to 30 people for two to five days. As a support guide, I assist the lead guide in carrying out these responsibilities and row the supply boat.

REFERENCES AVAILABLE

Patrick O'Callahan

1806 N. Washington Avenue, Apartment 362
Evansville, IN 47711-2298
Cell: (812) 555-2295
E-mail: Pat.OCallahan@xxx.com

Objective
Career in business administration management.

Education
North High School, Evansville, IN
Class of 2004
My course program has centered on a business and management
curriculum.

Specific courses include:
Business Law, Business Management, Economics, Accounting, Leader-
ship, Public Speaking, Psychology, Sociology, Personal Relationships, and
Japanese.

Communication Skills
- Completed three years of language arts courses, including Advanced
  Composition and Business Communications.
- Arranged and directed student discussion panel on global issues.
- Interacted successfully with the public in positions as a sales represen-
  tative and a part-time waiter.
- Served as campaign coordinator for successful student body presiden-
  tial candidate.
- Participated in debate team and forensics squad.
- Won two regional first place awards in debate and three second-place
  awards in persuasive speaking.

Leadership Skills
- Served two terms as student president for Junior Achievement.
- During that time membership increased 23 percent, and our organiza-
  tion was named best in the state.
- Established subcommittees to target membership drives and continue
  organizational development.

- Served as treasurer of Future Business Leaders of America, Evansville Regional Chapter.
- Coordinated joint activities among Bosse, Central, Harrison, North, and Reitz High Schools.
- Coordinated business career fair at city convention center.
- Worked with committee chairs to coordinate school visitations to promote business to junior high schools.

Experience

Sales Representative, Summers 2002–2004
Prange's Department Store, Boys Sportswear
Supervisor: Joey Ableman

Waiter, May 2001–June 2002
The Fish House
Supervisor: Annette Townsend

References

Available on request.

LEANDRO JUAREZ

1415 Wenig Road N.E. • Cedar Rapids, Iowa 52402
(319) 555-2284 • Leandro_Juarez@xxx.com

OCCUPATIONAL OBJECTIVE

To obtain an entry-level position with a computer software manufacturer in which my skills in computer programming and applications might lead to advancement in program design.

EDUCATIONAL BACKGROUND

Metro High School, Cedar Rapids, Iowa
Current Status: Senior
Computer Science GPA: 4.0
Cumulative GPA: 3.66

COMPUTER EXPERTISE

• Completed three semesters of computer programming.
• Developed programming projects individually and in teams.
• Proficient in BASIC, PASCAL, and C++ programming languages.
• Initiated self-study FORTRAN program project.
• Familiar with word processing, spreadsheet, and database programs.
• Knowledge of desktop publishing and graphic design software.
• Highly experienced with MS and Mac operating platforms.
• Basic knowledge of UNIX-based systems.
• Worked on special three-month project using NEXT computer system.

WORK HISTORY

Administrative Assistant, Health Care Nursing Center, June 2002 to present. Serve as swing-shift assistant manager for 60-bed facility. Supervise maintenance personnel. Also responsible for some support services, including patient form processing, database management, record keeping, and filing.

Young Men's Christian Association, September 2001 to June 2002. Supervised various evening recreational activities in facility that included swimming pool, shuffleboard, Ping-Pong, bowling lanes, and a gymnasium. Responsible for equipment check-out and locker room inspections.

EXTRACURRICULAR ACTIVITIES
- Vice President, Keyboard Club (member since 2001; V.P. 2002 to 2003)
- Peer tutor, mathematics
- Student Empowerment Training Project (STEP)
- Leadership Training Honors
- YMCA Youth of the Month, June 2002
- Computer Programming Award, Science VII Regional Competition
- National Honor Society Scholar of the Month, May 2003

References available on request.

Asher Toppman

10220 Goodwood Boulevard • Baton Rouge, LA 70802
(504) 555-8820 • AsherToppman@xxx.com

Career Objective
To become an efficient and effective legal assistant while beginning preparations for entering college pre-law program.

Education
Broadmoor High School, Baton Rouge, LA
Current status: Senior
GPA: 3.98

Leadership
- President, Associated Student Body of Broadmoor High School, 2003-2004
- Junior Class President, BHS, 2002-2003
- Sophomore Class Vice President, BHS, 2001-2002
- Freshman Student Senate Representative
- President, Forensics Team, 2001-2002
- News Director, Radio Club, 2000-2003

Communication
- Completed six semesters in writing and communication courses.
- Presented numerous speeches in forensics competition.
- Presented campaign speeches for elected offices.
- Won Young Democrats of America essay contest, 2002.
- Completed exploratory honors project in radio broadcasting.
- Served as news director for weekly 15-minute radio show on WBTR, produced by radio club.

Organization
- Directed planning and execution of several student events while serving as student body president and junior class president.
- Served on student senate ethics committee, which sponsored Honor Day and a "drug-free zone" day.
- Developed editorial procedures for planning weekly news broadcasts with other radio club officers. Honors
- Kiwanis Club Scholarship Designee, 2003
- Honors Program, Best Project Award, 2002
- Merit Scholar, Broadmoor PTA, 2001-2003

References are available on request.

Tristan Swanson

19 Malta Street
Augusta, Maine 04330
tristanswanson@xxx.com

Objective

A career in media communications in which my writing and editorial skills will be utilized to advantage.

Education

Cony High School, Augusta, Maine
Graduated: 2005
Major: Journalism and Communications

Writing Experience

- Activities and Entertainment Editor, *Cony Crier*, student newspaper, junior year.
- Wrote monthly column for local city newspaper, *Kennebec Journal*, High School page.
- Worked as reporter for the *Cony Crier* since freshman year.
- Completed two years of specialized course work in journalism and media communications.
- Wrote script for documentary film on ocean pollution on the Eastern Seaboard.
- Won publication of two poems in National Young Poets '03 competition, Boston, MA.

Leadership Experience

- Served as social committee chairman for student body of Cony High School.
- Planned various social events such as dances, barbecues, pep rallies, and a speaker's forum.
- Active in Letterman's Club, a service club of varsity sports players.
- Organized food drives and raffle to benefit Hunger Project.
- Captain, Varsity Basketball Team. Responsible for encouraging players in pre-game and post-practice activities.

Work History

Bath Cove Fleet, Bath, Maine. Summers 2002-2004.
Worked on a fishing boat as cook's helper and crew member.

Burger King, Augusta, Maine. September 2001-May 2002.
Worked part-time as kitchen staff and line cook while attending school.

References are available on request.

ALLISON BARNES

2880 West Braddock Road
Alexandria, VA 22302
Cell: (703) 555-1283
E-mail: AllisonBarnes@xxx.com

CAREER OBJECTIVE

To obtain a position with a small theater company in which my background in theater will allow me to make contributions in a variety of areas.

EXPERIENCE

- Directed production of Arthur Miller's *Death of a Salesman*. Took play to state drama competition and received honorable mention.
- Played Lisl in Community Theatre production of *The Sound of Music*. Won the part from among 84 auditioners.
- Designed sets and costumes, and worked on costume and set building crews, for a production of Shakespeare's *Twelfth Night*.
- Sang the lead in *Oklahoma*.
- Played a walk-on part in *Our Town*. Served backstage as key grip.
- Assisted with design and production of lighting for *Faculty Follies*, an entirely student-directed production starring teachers, counselors, and administrators from throughout the high school.
- Operated video cameras during dress rehearsals for *Our Town* and *Twelfth Night*.
- Wrote reviews of local theater (non-school) productions for student newspaper. One review was published in the weekend edition of the *Alexandria Gazette*.

EDUCATION

Williams Senior High School, Alexandria, VA
Class of 2004

COURSES:
Drama, Advanced Drama, Play Writing

SPECIAL PROJECTS:
Theater, Shakespeare, Creative Writing, Advanced Composition, and Journalism

WORK HISTORY

Waitress, New Morning Cafe, Alexandria, VA
January 2002-present

REFERENCES

Available on request

★ *Michael Newport*

2200 River Road, No. 126 • Annapolis, MD 21401
(301) 555-8461 • Mike-Newport@xxx.com

★ *Professional Goal*

To obtain an entry-level position in the news department of a daily newspaper in which I can utilize my journalism skills and professionalism.

★ *Education*

Broadneck Senior High School
1265 Green Holly Drive, Annapolis, MD
Class of 2004

★ *Writing Experience*

Student Reporter, *The BSHS Times*, Broadneck High School, 2000-present
★ Wrote articles on student government, administrative decisions, school board meetings, student activities, sports events, and profiles of student leaders and teachers.
★ Entered copy on computer word processing software. Served one semester as interim editor, determined story assignments for student reporters, worked with advisor on writing editorials, and edited news copy submitted by student reporters.
★ Served as staff photographer on several occasions.

Freelance Writer, 2003 to present
★ Published two articles in the "Teen Beat" section of the *Annapolis Daily Newspaper*.
★ Published one personality profile of the high school principal in *American Teen* magazine.
★ Submitted several query letters and manuscripts to a variety of magazines for publication.

★ *Activities*

★ Junior Press Club of Annapolis (a local high school division of the Maryland Press Club)
★ *The Lancer*, Broadneck SHS student annual (helped with photography, layout, editing); Aperture (photography club)

References and portfolio of writing and photography are available on request or online: www.MichaelNewport.com/portfolio

SUZANNE BARSTOW

2248 W. Billtown Road, Apt. 16 • Louisville, KY 40215
(502) 555-7751 • SuzanneBarstow@xxx.com

JOB OBJECTIVE

A part-time position as nurse's assistant in a hospital or health care facility. My long-term career goal is to become a pediatrician.

EXPERIENCE

Candy Striper, Louisville General Hospital
Volunteer 2000-present
Duties: Assist nurses with distribution of medication, visit with patients, deliver reading materials and other items at patient's request, provide general assistance to nursing staff.

EDUCATION

Iriquois High School, Taylor Boulevard, Louisville, KY
Class of 2005
Major: Health and Physical Education
GPA: 3.89
Courses Completed: Anatomy and Physiology, Basic Health, Personal Health and Wellness, CPRFirst Aid, Childhood Development, Advanced Foods and Nutrition.

COMMUNICATION SKILLS

- Completed three semesters of courses that specialized in written and oral business communication.
- Served as school spirit committee chair.
- Built sense of school spirit by establishing pep section for all athletic events.
- Coordinated with school band and rally squads to encourage participation.
- Participated for two semesters in forensics, presenting a variety of speeches on topics ranging from personal health and fitness to political issues.

Page 1 of 2

INTERPERSONAL SKILLS

- Attentive listener, able to lend a sympathetic, nonjudgmental ear when needed.
- Able to gain trust and rapport with various types of individuals.
- Concerned and empathetic, willing to help those in need.

HONORS

- Member of the National Honor Society.
- Selected Candy Striper of the Month, Louisville General Hospital.
- Placed second in state forensics competition, exposition category.

REFERENCES AVAILABLE ON REQUEST

MARY ALICE SIMPSON

1280 Delaware Avenue, Apt 116
Buffalo, NY 24214
(716) 555-8482
maryalicesimpson@xxx.com

OBJECTIVE

I am seeking an internship with a business enterprise in which
my skills in writing and communication may contribute to
the effectiveness of the organization.

EDUCATION

Holy Angels Academy, 24 Shoshane Street, Buffalo, NY
Class of 2004
GPA: 3.38

COURSE OF STUDY

My high school curriculum has offered me a broad background in
liberal studies and business in preparation for attending college. In
addition to course work in business, management, and accounting,
I participated in the college preparatory honors program, which
offered intensive courses in U.S. and European History, English
Composition, Research Methods, and Social Studies.

ACHIEVEMENTS AND ACTIVITIES

- Selected to serve as senior monitor for academic testing programs.
- Served on student government committee for finance.
- Conducted several successful campaigns to raise funds for school programs.
- Participated in the *a capella* choir, madrigal singers, and concert choir.
- Assisted with parent night preparations and planning.
- Member of the *Quill* staff, which published a school literary magazine.
- Published three poems in *Quill*.

References available upon request.

Tamar Sutterby

2404 Gallant Road
Charlotte, NC 28216

(704) 555-2119
TammySutterby@xxx.com

Objective

To obtain a position as a receptionist or clerical specialist.

Education

Central High School, Charlotte, NC
Graduated: June 2005

Courses taken:
Keyboarding Skill Building (65 wpm)
Computer Applications
Business Machines
Word Processing
Business Communications

Experience

Clerical Assistant, Central High School, Charlotte, NC
January-March 2002

> Worked with office staff as part of cooperative work experience program for class credit. Enhanced office and business skills through on-the-job learning.

> Duties included filing, typing, answering telephones, and serving as front desk receptionist.

Cashier, Wendy's Restaurant, Charlotte, NC
June-August 2001

> Worked front line cashier station and drive-through window. Greeted customers, collected prepared food according to orders, handled money, balanced cash drawer.

Activities

Ski Club, Young Republicans of North Carolina, Pep Club, Varsity Wrestling, Rally, Drama Club, Girls Choir

References available on request

ROBIN WEISS

2250 Second Avenue
Akron, OH 44313
(216) 555-9941
RobinWeiss@xxx.com

JOB SOUGHT

Sales clerk with sporting goods or department store.

EDUCATION

Firestone High School, Akron, OH
Class of 2004

EXPERIENCE

Sales clerk, Firestone Student Store, September 2000–present.
• Operated student store sales. Handled cash exchanges and credit account charges.
• Balanced daily receipts.

Referee, Summit County Soccer Clubs, 2001–2003.
• Served as referee for elementary and junior high school–level soccer games.

SPECIAL SKILLS

• Trained in CPR and advanced lifesaving
• Fluent in Spanish
• Knowledgeable about a wide variety of outdoor sports

ACTIVITIES

• Recreational Water Sports Club
• Outdoor School Counselor
• Explorers Club

REFERENCES

Available on request

Brenda Pitt-Williams

3488 Chester Avenue
Philadelphia, Pennsylvania 19151
(215) 555-7741
Brendapitt-williams@xxx.com

Objective

Nurse's Aide in health care organization.

Education

Friends Central School
North 68th and City Avenue
Philadelphia, PA
Graduated: 2002

Abilities

Trained in CPR and emergency first aid.
Experienced in working with invalids.
Completed coursework in human anatomy and physiology.
Studied nutrition and stress management.
Worked with children involved in crisis intervention.
Experienced in maintaining antiseptic environment.

Experience

Volunteer, Cheltenham Nursing Home, 2000 to present.
Visit with elderly invalids. Read letters and newspapers to those who need assistance. Help maintenance staff. Assist nursing staff with rounds and distribution of food trays.

Volunteer, Women's Shelter, operated by the Friends Society, 2001 to 2003. Helped children of women staying at the shelter adjust to changes. Gathered donations of toys and games and played with children of all ages.

Baby-sitter, various private individuals, 1999 to present.
Provide child care for several children, from three months to twelve years of age. Have cared for as many as seven children at a time.

Activities

- Scholarship and Leadership Committee
- Volunteer Assistance League Friends for Peaceful Conflict Resolution, Junior Chapter
- Study Session Leader Peer Tutor, English and History

References are available upon request.

Burke Anderson

260 E. North Avenue
Baltimore, Maryland 21202
(301) 555-4458
burkeanderson@xxx.com

Objective

A career in technology design and development that will utilize my skills in technology innovation and traditional and computer-aided drafting.

Education

Baltimore City High School, Baltimore, Maryland
Major: science and technology
GPA in major: 6.0 (scale of 6); cumulative GPA: 4.85

Accomplishments

• Tied for Best of Show in regional competition, Technology Challenge '02, held at Massachusetts Institute of Technology, for the design and construction of a hovercraft.
• Qualified for competition in Technology Challenge '03 with the design and construction of a solar-powered remote-controlled sailboat.

Completed the following course work:
• Drafting 1-4
• Metal Technology
• Electricity/Electronics
• Wood Technology
• Computer-Aided Drafting
• Design and Technology
• 1-2 Career Mechanics
• AutoCAD

Participated in Cooperative Work Experience projects in drafting and career mechanics.

Work Experience

Drafting Intern, Cardell Associates, Baltimore, Maryland, Summer 2004.
Duties: Checked blueprints of CAD-drafted plans for parts and equipment manufactured by Cardell. Drafted initial drawings of existing parts that required changes to fit new machinery.

Mechanics Intern, East Baltimore Auto, Baltimore, Maryland, Summer 2003.
Duties: Worked as assistant mechanic for import cars. Learned diagnostics procedures and equipment operation.

Activities

• Techies, BCHS Technology Club
• Young Sailors of Baltimore
• Radio Club
• Youth Draftsmen Club

References and portfolio of drafting projects available on request.

Bruce C. Cantrell

120 Border Street
Hot Springs, Arkansas 71901
Telephone: (501) 555-7367
brucecantrell@xxx.com

OBJECTIVE

Summer internship with company doing business with international import
and export trade.

EDUCATION

Lakeside Senior High School, Malvern Road, Hot Springs, Arkansas
Graduated: 2004
Major: Business

Specialized Courses: Business series courses in Accounting and Management, Marketing, Japanese I and II, Economics, Introduction to Statistics.
GPA: 3.9

Special Projects: Developed three-year business finance, development and
marketing plan for simulated business. In economics, made most significant
profit margin from series of planned investments.

WORK EXPERIENCE

Garland County Exposition Center, May–September 2004
Hot Springs, Arkansas
Work Crew Supervisor: Morgan Stewart
Duties: Worked during summer exhibition season. Responsibilities included
grounds maintenance, ticket selling, livestock herding and registration, and
event preparation.

Newspaper Delivery, Sentinel-Record, September 2000–May 2003
Hot Springs, Arkansas
Supervisor: Walter E. Ballentine Jr.

Lakeside Senior High School Grounds Crew, June 1999–September 2000
Supervisor: Connie Lofstedt

ACTIVITIES

• Future Business Leaders of America, Hot Springs
• Junior Achievement
• Junior Class Treasurer

References are available on request.

Brittany Schoonover

318 S.E. 151st Street • Eugene, Oregon 97405

(503) 555-6246 • Brittany_Schoonover@xxx.com

Education
South Eugene High School, Eugene, Oregon. Graduated: 2005

Skills
- Typing (55 wpm)
- Strong writing skills
- Computer keyboarding (70 wpm)
- Business communications training
- Ten-key adding machine (40 wpm)
- Business systems training
- MS Office
- Webpage Design

Work Experience
Data entry, State of Oregon Human Resources Division, Eugene, Oregon 97233 June–August 2004
Duties: transferred data from handwritten forms onto computer forms, checked data entries for accuracy and made needed corrections, and sorted and filed computer printouts.

Activities
- Peer tutor in language arts
- Rally squad, junior varsity basketball
- Social events program committee
- Library assistance league
- School literary magazine editorial committee

References
Available on request

Melinda W. Adams

810 N. 1430 Del Rio Drive
Tempe, Arizona 85282
(503) 555-9530
melinda@xxx.com

Objective

Seeking summer employment in retail sales that will continue as part-time employment during the school year.

Education

Corona Del Sol High School. Graduated: 2005.

Courses: Computer Applications, Word Processing, Office Management, Math, and Business

Work Experience

Office Assistant, Dave Whitehead Insurance Company, September 2004–present
Duties: answer telephones, assist clients, answer questions about insurance claims, fill out claim forms, operate office machines, perform word processing, and file.

Cashier and Hostess, Judie's Chicken Haven, Lakeshore Drive, June–September 2004
Duties: greeted and seated customers, assisted waitresses and busboys with clearing and setting tables, entered sales in cash register, made change.

Achievements

- Volleyball and basketball team member; Volleyball Player of the Year 2004
- First flute soloist, concert orchestra
- Jazz ensemble
- Drill team; served as captain 2002–2004
- Music Appreciation Club Member

References

Available on request

KARIN BOWLES

2050 Crown Boulevard, Apt. C • Denver, CO 80204
(303) 555-2280 • karinbowles@xxx.com

GOAL

A career in business administration.

EXPERIENCE

LEADERSHIP

As a member of the finance committee for the Associated Students of Kennedy High School, I supervised the planning and execution of school-wide fund-raising projects such as candy sales and the student carnival. I also set meeting dates and presided over meetings, reported to student council, and worked with the student government advisor on budgeting.

COMMUNICATION

Worked on the publicity committees for several student events and election campaigns. Wrote text for fliers and signs and assisted with speech writing. Each campaign ended in election victory for my candidate.

Completed two semesters of business communications courses. Also completed three years of honors-level English composition and three years of French. Have working knowledge of spoken and written French.

ORGANIZATION

Served as assistant librarian, a position usually held by a paid professional, during the semester prior to graduation. Directed a research methods seminar for freshman students. Answered questions about library reference materials and on-line research sources. Supervised student workers in shelving books. Updated computerized database.

EDUCATION

Kennedy High School, 2855 Lamar Street, Denver, CO
September 2000-June 2004

Pertinent Courses: Business Law, Accounting, Computer Applications in Business, Office Procedures, Word Processing, Business Management.

REFERENCES

Available on request.

Jennifer Smith

345 Forest Street
Dover, Delaware 19901
(302) 555-5835
jennifersmith@xxx.com

Job Sought

Classroom assistant position in preschool, day care center, or elementary school.

Relevant Experience

Dover Elementary School
Supervisor: Mrs. Wilkerson

Duties: Worked for one semester as part of exploratory education experience class. Assisted kindergarten teacher with supervision of students on playground and during classroom activities. Read stories and directed group activities. Taught songs and rhythm.

Education

September 2000–June 2004
Dover High School, Walker Road, Dover, Delaware

September 1997–June 2000
Dover Air Force Base Middle School, Hawthorne Drive, Dover, Delaware

Exploring Childhood I and II, Human Development, First Aid and Safety, Basic Health

Work History

June 2003–present
Clerk, Dover AFB Commissary
Assist with stocking and daily preparation.

References available on request.

Judith Fritch

16047 E. Bentsen, Apartment 25
Portland, Oregon 97223
(503) 555-5121
judithfritch@xxx.com

◆ Objective

To obtain a part-time clerical job in a city or county government office in which I can utilize my office management skills.

◆ Skills

Professional attitude
Organized
10-key adding machine
Reliable
Typing 60 wpm
Responsible
Self-starter
Filing

◆ Education

I am currently a senior at Central High School, Bay City, Oregon, with an expected graduation date of June 2005.

Graduation seminar project: currently involved in preparing an in-depth report on business management systems and operations in city and county government offices.

◆ Experience

Receptionist, Thrifty Auto Leasing, July 2002-January 2004
456 Central Boulevard, Bay City, Oregon
Duties: Managed telephone switchboard, assisted clients, directed clients to appropriate department, typed letters, typed auto leasing forms, filed, assisted sales staff.

◆ References

Available on request

Kenneth Zimmerman
Route 32, Box 2216 • Central Valley, NY 10917
(914) 555-4481 • Ken_Zimmerman@xxx.com

Objective

A position with a political action organization working for social improvement.

Education

Monroe-Woodbury High School, Central Valley, NY
Graduated: 2005.

Skills & Achievement

• Experienced with a variety of computer software and hardware, including Word on Mac and IBM.
• Experienced with providing customer service.
• Trained in basic bookkeeping, invoicing, inventory, and payroll procedures.
• Served as vice president of Associated Students of Monroe-Woodbury High School, founder and president of Students for Global Awareness, director of one-act play for student drama presentation.
• Excellent writing and communications skills.
• Wrote and presented several speeches during all-school election campaign.
• Ran on platform of working to improve student awareness of global issues.

Employment History

Sales Assistant, Video Circle, Chester, NY
June-September 2003.
Duties: Provided assistance to customers in video sales and rental store. Worked with database on IBM-compatible computer system. Handled cash and credit card transactions. Maintained accurate inventory system.

References

Available on request.

MARY JO AZUKAS

14 West 22nd Street • Trenton, NJ 08602
(609) 555-3477
maryjoazukas@xxx.com

Objective

To obtain a position as assistant manager in a small restaurant.

Experience

Head Cashier, Burgerville USA
September 2003-present

Duties: Supervise cashier staff during evening shift. Check balance sheets at end of shift. Work counter and drive-through window as needed.

Line Cook/Cashier, Tony's Burger Emporium
June 2002-August 2003

Duties: Greeted customers, took orders, helped kitchen crew prepare meals and drinks, assisted with maintaining stock, cleaning, and closing procedures. Responsible for having balanced till after each shift.

Education

Capitol High School-Trenton, NJ
Class of 2005

Honors

• Cashier of the Month, Burgerville USA, February 2004
• Junior Cheerleader of the Year, 2004
• "Cappy" Award for best supporting actress in a student production, 2003

References are available on request.

ANTOINETTE RUPERT
238 ORANGE STREET
TAMPA, FL 33606
(813) 555-3953
ANTOINETTERUPERT@XXX.COM

OBJECTIVE
To become part of the support services team for a small but growing business.

EDUCATION
Hillhouse Central High School, 480 Sherman Parkway, New Haven, CT
Graduated: June 2004.

Concentration: Accounting I and II, Computer Applications I and II (word processing, spreadsheet, database, design, page layout, and communications software for Windows operating system), Business Management, and Business Communications.

EXPERIENCE
Temporary Clerical Worker, Kelly Services, 2003-present

Duties: Work for a wide range of clients, including a bank, mortgage trust company, supply warehouse, architectural office, city government office, and law office. Duties have included typing, filing, answering telephones, preparing forms, computer data entry, transcribing dictation, and general office assistance.

ACTIVITIES & ACHIEVEMENTS
• Secretary, Junior Class HCHS, 2003-2004
• Assistant Editor, *HCHS Yearbook*, 2002-2003
• Secretary, Future Business Leaders of America, 2001-2002
• Member, Student Recycling Committee, 2003-2004
• Member, HCHS Camera Club, 2000-2004

References are available on request.

PAUL JEROME

412 Lincoln Road
Las Vegas, NV 87701
(505) 555-6623
pauljerome@xxx.com

OBJECTIVE

Seeking summer employment on the restaurant staff of a large hotel. Long-term goal: a career in hotel and restaurant management.

EDUCATION

South High School, 300 Chesterfield Avenue, Las Vegas, NV, Class of 2005.

EXPERIENCE

Busboy, Denny's Restaurant, Las Vegas, NV. September 2004–present.
Duties: Assist waitresses with serving meals, clear and set tables, serve beverages.

Grounds Crew, Circus Circus, Las Vegas, NV. June–August 2004.
Duties: Trimmed hedges, replaced indoor and outdoor plants, operated irrigation system, kept walkways and grounds clean, assisted with pool maintenance.

Maintenance Crew, Caesar's Palace, Las Vegas, NV.
June–August 2003.
Duties: Maintained regular schedule of pool maintenance, assisted with janitorial responsibilities, worked with grounds crew on landscape maintenance, provided some assistance with equipment repair.

REFERENCES AVAILABLE

Tony Pomeroy

2307 N. Broad Street • Philadelphia, PA 19119 • (215) 555-2258
Tony_Pomeroy@xxx.com

Objective

A staff position as a photographer or darkroom technician on a newspaper or magazine.

Education

Northeast Prep School, Cottman Avenue, Philadelphia, PA
Class of 2004
Course emphases: Journalism, Photojournalism, Photography 1-3, Darkroom (beginning and advanced), Digital Photography, Digital Image Correction, Computer Applications in Art

Relevant Skills & Experience

- Completed projects in following fields: black-and-white 35mm photography, photo silkscreen and offset printing, computer alteration of photographic imagery (using Digital Darkroom on Macintosh computer), digital image enhancement and color correction.
- Won first place in *Philadelphia Daily News* amateur photo contest, high school category. Photo published in July 2004 edition.
- Completed photo essay for submission to regional amateur photo contest sponsored by Kodak. (Results as yet undetermined.)
- Operated copy camera for making PMTs and halftone screens.
- Completed extracurricular project on 35mm color photography.

Work History

Northeast Prep Student Newspaper Photo Editor, 2003-2004
Staff Photographer, 2001-2002

- Supervised student photography staff.
- Selected photographs for publication from analysis of negative or contact sheets.
- Assigned photography projects and maintained check-out of school cameras.
- Shot, developed, and printed photographs.

Extracurricular Activities

- Camera Club
- President, Brush and Easel (art student association)

PORTFOLIO AND REFERENCES AVAILABLE ONLINE
www.tonypomeroy.com/portfolio

Timothy J. Davison

1286 West Shore Road, Apt. 5
Warwick, RI 02889
(402) 555-2117
timothydavison@xxx.com

Objective

A position as chef's assistant at a restaurant featuring specialty or gourmet cuisine.

Education

The Culinary Institute
114 First Avenue, New York, NY 10019
Video correspondence course, to be completed December 2005.

Taft Senior High School
575 Centerville Road, Warwick, RI 02886
Class standing: Junior

Special Skills

Worked with International Student Club to plan and prepare a meal for 250 parents and students. Involved with menu planning and food preparation for dishes from all over the world.

Catered a dinner party for six people as part of a donation of services to raise funds for local Boys and Girls Club. Prepared and helped serve five-course dinner.

Completed one year of culinary video correspondence course that involved preparation of primarily French cuisine. Although not required by course, I have followed a procedure of preparing the lesson plan menu for a group of four to six people who provide a written evaluation of the meal and its presentation.

Work Experience

Kitchen Prep Staff, June 2003–present
Warwick Towers Restaurant
34 Warwick Lake Avenue, Warwick, RI 02889

References are available on request.

Toby Waterson

200 South Third Avenue   (213) 555-9226
Arcadia, CA 91006   tobywaterson@xxx.com

Objective
A position with the technical department of a manufacturing company.

Experience
Technical Design
❖ Designed and built solar-powered car (one-person).
❖ Designed multi-media computer-directed light and sound presentation.
❖ Developed model for automated, solar-powered home.
❖ Completed two years of design and technology program.

Engine Mechanics
❖ Built motor for solar-powered car.
❖ Assisted with engine rebuilding on two Volkswagens.
❖ Assisted in engine repair on riding and other lawn mowers.

Work History
Grounds Crew/Maintenance, June 2003-present
Riverview Apartments, Arcadia, CA
Duties: landscape maintenance, some plumbing, carpentry, general repair.

Library Assistant, 2002-2003
Foothills Junior High School, Arcadia, CA
Duties: audio-visual equipment repair, office work, reshelving, data entry.

Education
Arcadia Senior High School, Class of 2002
Major: Design and Technology

References
Available on request.

JASMINE PARKER

4223 Kilauea Avenue
P.O. Box 2214
Honolulu, HI 96819
Phone: (818) 555-2294
jasmineparker@xxx.com

OBJECTIVE

To obtain a position in fisheries and wildlife management administration that
will utilize my skills in scientific research, analysis, and communication.

EDUCATION

Honolulu Community College, Dillingham Boulevard, Honolulu, HI
Enrolled in summer open enrollment programs, 2003 and 2004
Earned 3.6 GPA in science courses

Kaimuki High School, 2705 Kaimuka Avenue, Honolulu, HI
Graduated: 2004
Science GPA: 4.0. Cumulative GPA: 3.56

SCIENCE BACKGROUND

• Designed and conducted research project on underwater testing procedures
• Assisted with research project designed to decrease mercury toxicity
• Completed two years of general biology, including one college-level course
• Completed two semesters of marine biology, including one college-level course
• Completed one college-level course in scientific research methods
• Completed one college-level course in fisheries science

COMMUNICATIONS BACKGROUND

• Wrote report on fisheries management problems, presented at Science '03
• Completed four years of writing, including college-level course in technical
  writing
• Member, Kaimuki High School Forensics Club; presented several prepared
  speeches
• Winner, Honolulu Toastmasters Honorable Mention for presentation on
  science careers for women

REFERENCES AVAILABLE

Sandra G. Naylor

1415 NE San Rafael Street
Santa Cruz, CA 95061
(805) 555-0439
sandranaylor@xxx.com

EDUCATION   2003-present, Santa Cruz Senior High School, Santa Cruz, CA

1999-2002, Alvore School of Dance, San Francisco, CA

EXPERIENCE   Part-time receptionist, Dr. Jonathan Naylor, Santa Cruz, 2003-present

Answer telephones, call patients to remind them about appointments, schedule appointments, check patients in, assist with billing to insurance companies and patients, perform word processing, and file.

SKILLS   Experienced with office reception desk responsibilities
Computer word processing speed of 75 wpm
Knowledge of Word and Quicken
Shorthand speed of 90 wpm
Experienced with mail merge capabilities of computer word processing
Pleasant telephone manner
Basic website development using MS Front Page
Content management experience using Blogger and MoveableType

ACTIVITIES   Chair, Winterfest Committee Member
Homecoming Committee Dance Team
School musicals and plays
Softball Team

REFERENCES   Available upon request

Brandon Reaman

1147 N.E. 160th
Portland, Oregon 97230
(503) 555-1361
brandonreaman@xxx.com

Objective

Summer employment with construction crew.

Experience and Skills

My work experience includes assisting with roofing, building fences, and providing lawn and garden maintenance. I have worked for a private contractor to build a deck, remodel a kitchen, and reconstruct an 18 × 24–foot porch that had collapsed.

In a design and technology program, I worked with a team of three other students to design and build a balsa wood bridge that could support at least 50 pounds. Our design exceeded supporting 100 pounds.

Able to operate the following: lathe, table saw, drill press, compression hammer, and other metal and woodworking machinery.

Work History

Crew member, Red Hat Remodeling, June–September 2003.

Crew member, Johnson Construction, June–September 2002.

Education

Reynolds High School, 1698 S.W. Cherry Park Road, Troutdale, Oregon
Graduated: 2005

Relevant Coursework

Practical Physics, Woods II, Metals II, Building Construction, Design and Technology, Technical Drawing, Drafting, Computer Assisted Drawing (CAD)

References

Available upon request.

SHARON ANNE GILBERT

1735 N.E. Moore • Chattanooga, TN 37402
(615) 555-3374 • sharongilbert@xxx.com

EDUCATION

Howard High School, 2500 Market Street, Chattanooga, TN
Graduated: 2004
Major: Business

SKILLS

• Word processing, filing, organizing.
• Able to operate the following: IBM and Macintosh computers (various word processing programs), ten-key adding machine, postage meter.
• Have valid driver's license.

WORK EXPERIENCE

Child care provider. Mrs. Jolie Chappell (full-time, summers) and various other families (part-time, throughout the year). 2001-present.

Provide care for children of various ages. Responsible for feeding and observing nap time and bedtime routines. I am always careful to leave the house as I found it and to help the children gain a sense of responsibility about their environment.

ACTIVITIES

• Church choir and youth group
• Howard High Concert Choir Social Committee
• Student Government
• One year Symphony Orchestra

REFERENCES

Available on request.

STEPHEN P. DILLON

18445 S.W. Mirick Road • Denton, TX 76201
(817) 555-4550 • stephendillon@xxx.com

JOB OBJECTIVE

To secure a position on a carpentry crew for full-time summer employment.

EDUCATION

Denton Senior High School, 1007 Fulton Street, Denton, TX
Graduated: 2004

Related courses: Home Building Construction (PGE Good Sense Home), Woodshop I and II, Auto Technology. Maintained top grades in each of these courses.

WORK EXPERIENCE

Buzz Burton (private contractor), August 2003-present, as work is available.

    Completed deck construction project, washed and painted interior and exterior of buildings, built foundation forms. Assisted with framing and roofing.

Andersen Construction, September 2003.

    Stripped and refitted a kitchen according to code specifications; installed insulation; removed and replanted shrubbery.

Mose Brothers Concrete, summers of 2002 and 2003.

    Excavation crew member, worked on ditch-digging crew. Operated chain saw, jumping jack, trencher, backhoe, cat loader, and dump truck.

ACTIVITIES

Four years of wrestling, two years of football, assistant coach for girls' softball.

REFERENCES

Available upon request.

RAYMOND KELLER

1701 S. 29th Street • Sheboygan, WI 53082
(414) 555-1665 • raymondkeller@xxx.com

OBJECTIVE

Obtain position as apprentice mechanic in auto repair center.

EDUCATION

North High School, Sheboygan, WI
Graduated: 2005

COURSE TAKEN

Auto Mechanics 1 & 2
Career Mechanics
Principles of Technology
Metal Shop
Wood Shop
Design & Technology
Drafting
Electricity/Electronics

WORK EXPERIENCE

Shop Steward, Sheboygan North Auto Shop, 2003–present
Student-run auto center located at high school; run diagnostics,
estimate costs, supervise repairs

Station Attendant, Winnebago Garage, August 2002–present

Station Attendant, Four Towers Shell, 2001–2002

ACTIVITIES

Four years high school football, Letterman's Club, boating and fishing

References are available on request.

• *JERIANNE JONES*

1288 N.W. 58th Street • Seattle, Washington 98117
(206) 555-1941 • E-mail: jeriannejones@xxx.com

• *EDUCATION*

Ballard High School
Graduated: 2004

Lakeside Upper School, Seattle
Attended 2001-2003

• *EXPERIENCE*

Clerical: During the school year, I work in the school's central office as a clerical assistant. I type, operate various duplication machines for the teachers and secretaries, file, and deliver messages. I have received high reviews for each of the two years I have served as an assistant.

Counseling: In May 2002 and April 2003, I served as a counselor at the Bainbridge Island Outdoor School. I supervised the children on the buses and took them on discovery walks through the rain forest.

In the summers of 2001 and 2002, I spent several weeks as a YMCA camp counselor, teaching outdoor survival skills, canoeing, and swimming.

I hold an up-to-date advanced lifesaving certificate.

Volunteer: As a member of the student welfare committee, I planned a social awareness week that brought speakers from several Seattle social service agencies to speak at the high school.

I organized a food and clothing drive at Ballard High School for relief following earthquakes in Nicaragua and worked with a charitable organization to raise money for Romanian orphans.

• *ACHIEVEMENTS*

- Selected to present student essay on volunteerism at Lyons Club, Ballard Chapter.
- Worked on student yearbook staff as copy editor.
- Member of Associated Students of Ballard High School student welfare committee.

• *REFERENCES*

Available upon request.

JORY AHRENS

131 172nd Avenue N.E.
Bellevue, WA 98006
(206) 555-9027
joryahrens@xxx.com

OBJECTIVE
To obtain a retail sales position in women's clothing department or boutique. My long-range objective is a career in fashion merchandising.

EDUCATION
Sammamish High School, 469 148th Avenue S.W., Bellevue, WA
Graduated: 2005

WORK EXPERIENCE
Student Manager
SHS Athletics Shop, Sammamish High School, 2003 to 2004
> Worked with committee to select and purchase merchandise for student-run sports shop, which carries T-shirts and sweat shirts, rental equipment, and sporting goods. Supervised student workers, applied transfer designs to clothing, and oversaw budgeting and finance committee.

Sales Representative
Earrings Galore, 2000 to 2003
> Served customers, made sales, operated the cash register, and assisted with preparing window displays.

SKILLS
- Experienced with operating a cash register, Macintosh computer, scientific calculator, and ten-key adding machine.
- Keen eye for window displays and point-of-sale merchandising.

ACTIVITIES
- Served as a counselor at the Camp for the Blind.
- Member of International Club.
- Played three years of team volleyball.
- Work at school track meets.

REFERENCES
Available upon request.

JAMES JACKSON

4217 E. Washington Street
St. Louis, MO 63119
(314) 555-9487
jamesjackson@xxx.com

SUMMARY
Qualified for skilled carpentry position. Experienced in rough and finished carpentry, woodworking, furniture design and construction.

EDUCATION
Graduate, Local 7, International Carpenter's Union Apprenticeship Program

Graduate, Lincoln Vocational High School, St. Louis, MO, 2002

JOB EXPERIENCE
2003–present
Draftsman, Belle Architectural Inc., St. Louis, MO
Responsible for drafting and blueprint reading, construction of scale models for architects.

2000–2003
Assistant Manager, Blair Woodworking, St. Louis, MO
Assisted owner of precision woodworking shop with design and production of custom furniture using AutoCAD and Johnson Controlled CNC machines. Special order projects for home owners and builders.

REFERENCES
Business and personal references on request
Detailed photo portfolio available

Nicholas Vittaco

822 Hillside Drive
Brooklyn, New York 10036
(212) 555-8756
nicholasvittaco@xxx.com

Goal

Entry-level job as drafter for a local architectural firm.

Training

Graduate, McMurray Technical High School, 2004

Honors

• Voted Outstanding Senior by teachers and classmates
• GPA: 3.5/Honor Roll status

Work History

Construction Worker, Benson & Sons, Brooklyn, New York
Summers, 2000 - 2004

• Worked summer construction jobs throughout high school.
• Operated heavy equipment.
• Interpreted blueprints and other architectural drawings and instructions.
• Delivered building materials to job sites.
• Achieved rank of junior carpenter.

References will be provided upon request.

Marilyn Smith

418 Whitesburn Street
Wauconda, IL 60084
(847) 555-9822
marilynsmith@xxx.com

Objective   Nurse Assistant Position

Employment   2003 - present
Nurse Assistant, Pinkerton Nursing Center,
Wauconda, IL

Give report to RNs regarding status of patients and
current needs. Assist patients with bathing, groom-
ing needs. Monitor and record fluid intake and out-
put, vital signs, general changes in mood or
appearance. Promote mental and physical health of
patients while assisting nursing staff.

2001 - 2003
Office Assistant, Kusler Medical Group, Deerfield, IL

Maintained patient files, answered phones, scheduled appointments, typed correspondence. Provided
general clerical support for busy pediatric office.

Education   Nursing Assistant Certification, June 2003
Columbia Vocational Institute, Chicago, IL

Graduated: 2001
Wauconda High School, Wauconda, IL

References   Available on request

Chapter 6

Sample Cover Letters

This chapter contains sample cover letters for students and graduates who are pursuing a wide variety of jobs and careers.

There are many different styles of cover letters in terms of layout, level of formality, and presentation of information. These samples also represent people with varying amounts of education and work experience. Choose one cover letter or borrow elements from several different cover letters to help you construct your own.

JUAN AGUILAR

158 Halladay S.W.
Benton Harbor, MI 49028
Juan.Aguilar@xxx.com
(616) 555-7379

September 1, 20--

Mr. Charles Hensen
Production Manager
The Herald-Palladium
3450 Hollywood Road
St. Joseph, MI 49085

Dear Mr. Hensen:

Mr. George Petersen of Michigan Printing suggested I contact you with regard to my enthusiastic interest in a career in the printing industry. I would like to apply for a position as an apprentice printer and have enclosed my resume for your consideration.

This past summer I worked for Mr. Petersen as a print shop assistant. As the summer vacation relief worker, I was able to move throughout the printing department, and in the process I learned a tremendous amount about the trade. In addition, my course work in graphic arts and computer applications has given me a background that will be very useful in mastering electronic prepress techniques.

I would very much appreciate an opportunity to talk with you and see the printing operations at the newspaper. Mr. Petersen spoke very highly of the production department, and I hope to become part of your team. I will call you within the next few days, or you may reach me at the above number most afternoons.

Sincerely,

Juan Aguilar

JASON RAINTREE

2268-A 187th Street
Seattle, WA 98055
(206) 555-9225

September 20, 20--

Mr. Henry B. Thurston
Assistant to the Director
Washington Children's Services Division
220 W. First Avenue
Seattle, WA 98022

Dear Mr. Thurston:

I am writing to apply for an internship with the Washington Children's Services Division. I understand from my child development instructor, Susan Bishop, that you have four such positions available each summer.

My educational training in child development and psychology has already been beneficial in programs I have been involved with. I have become especially interested in carrying anti-drug and alcohol messages to young people. Toward this end, I worked with the Boys and Girls Club of South Seattle and started a club at Tyee High School, "Tyee (Naturally) High Club," which has stirred a tremendous response among students.

I will be happy to serve CSD in whatever capacity I may be the most useful. I have a variety of skills in addition to those listed on my resume. Specifically, I am familiar with computer word processing and am quite skilled at general clerical work. I would like to speak with you at your convenience about your expectations for the student intern and how I might best contribute to CSD's efforts. My telephone number is 555-9225, and I am generally at home in the early morning and late afternoon.

Sincerely,

Jason Raintree

ROBERT GOLDSTEIN

2250 Collins Avenue

Huntington, West Virginia 25702

Bob.Goldstein@xxx.com

(304) 555-9941

June 26, 20--

Mr. Frank Westerman
Fire Chief
Huntington Fire District
680 Temple Avenue
Huntington, WV 25702

Dear Mr. Westerman:

I was delighted to see your advertisement for firefighter trainees in yesterday's *Herald Dispatch* because it has been my lifelong ambition to become a firefighter. My resume is enclosed for your review.

My activities and course work in high school have centered on health, physical fitness, and sports. I have maintained excellent physical condition, which your advertisement indicates is a must for prospective firefighters. I have also had advanced training in first aid and CPR.

Once you have had an opportunity to review my resume, I will call to set up an appointment at your convenience to further discuss my interests and qualifications. I am eager to pursue a career in fire prevention and protection.

Sincerely,

Robert Goldstein

MASOUD YASMIR ◆ ◆ ◆

211 South Grevillea Avenue, Apt. 26B
Inglewood, CA 90301
M.Yasmir@xxx.com
(213) 555-9562

May 15, 20--

J. E. Davis
Stanton Electronics
2516 West Palm Drive, Suite 116
Laguna Beach, CA 92653

Dear J. E. Davis:

In reply to your recent advertisement in the *Times*, I have enclosed my resume for consideration in your search for an electronics technician.

I believe my training and experience provide me with the background you are looking for. My work in the design and manufacturing of radar-controlled devices will allow me to immediately take on the challenges of Stanton Electronics. I have extensive knowledge of circuitry and electronic soldering and would like to apply those skills to greater challenges.

I look forward to having an opportunity to visit your facilities and talk with you about the projects I have completed. I will be happy to bring some of the more relevant of these in order for you to see the quality of my work and the innovation in the designs. My number is (213) 555-9562, and I may be reached most mornings.

Thank you for your consideration.

Sincerely,

Masoud Yasmir

3836 Sweetwater Avenue
Scottsdale, AZ 85254

May 6, 20--

Carol Emory
Emory & Associates
One West Monroe, Suite 2017
Phoenix, AZ 85004

Dear Ms. Emory:

I am writing to request the opportunity to work for you as a summer intern. I understand from my adviser at Stanford University that your firm often takes on summer interns.

I will graduate from Chaparral High School in Scottsdale this month and will enter Stanford's pre-law program in September. I hope to use my summer to learn more about private legal practice by working in whatever way I might best contribute to your firm.

As the enclosed resume indicates, I am a hard worker who takes pride in doing the best possible job at every task I take on. I hold a 4.0 grade point average and will graduate in the top five percent of my class. I have experience in clerical work, and I am willing to put in the long hours that are standard for anyone involved in legal practice.

I would like to arrange a time to visit with you at your convenience to learn more about how I can contribute my abilities. My telephone number is (602) 555-2834, and I am available after 3:30 daily.

Yours sincerely,

Paul Garcia

Michael Han

435 South Monaco Parkway
Denver, Colorado 80204
(303) 555-4481
michaelhan@xxx.com

February 15, 20--

Mr. John Seward
Seward and Whitely, CPAs
21 West Riddlington
Denver, Colorado 80216

Dear Mr. Seward:

I am responding to the February 10 advertisement in the *Post* announcing openings for part-time temporary accounting clerks. My resume is enclosed for your review.

As my resume indicates, I have received extensive training in accounting and bookkeeping and am familiar with several computer software programs that deal with accounting, including Excel and Access spreadsheets. Working for your company would be a timely opportunity to put these skills to the challenge of aiding your firm during the tax season. Upon graduation, I hope to pursue a college degree in accounting.

I would appreciate an opportunity to meet with you, at your convenience, to discuss the position. The advertisement indicated that hours are flexible, and as I am still in school, I would be available to work any day after 2:00 p.m. and could extend my hours as long as necessary to accomplish the job. I may be reached at 555-4481 any afternoon.

Thank you for your consideration. I look forward to talking with you.

Sincerely,

Michael Han

JUDY REIMER

128 Orange Street • New Haven, CT 06510
(203) 555-3754 • judyreimer@xxx.com

April 26, 20--

Ms. Verna Howard
Office Manager
Benson, Keller, Harcourt, and Vinson, Attorneys at Law
12 Front Avenue, Suite 1200
New Haven, CT 06508

Dear Ms. Howard:

I am enclosing a resume and letters of recommendation, submitted in response to your advertisement for a paralegal assistant that appeared in the April 20th *New Haven Gazette*.

I will graduate with highest honors from Hillhouse High School next month following a four-year curriculum centered on business, law, and office management. I believe my training and my previous experience as an office assistant for the firm of Switter, Harvey, Jenkins & Hewitt have prepared me for assuming the responsibilities of a paralegal assistant.

I would appreciate the opportunity to meet with you at your convenience. I am eager to put my skills to work for your firm. I may be reached at 555-3754 in the afternoons.

Thank you for considering my application.

Yours truly,

Judy Reimer

Mary Jo Baptiste
2240 N.W. Nebraska Avenue
Washington, DC 20016
(202) 555-7465
maryjobaptiste@xxx.com

May 28, 20--

Ms. Belinda Summers, Director
Jefferson Montessori School
620 N.W. Jefferson Avenue
Washington, DC 20018

Dear Ms. Summers:

I would like to put forward my application for the summer program guide position at Jefferson Montessori, advertised in Sunday's *City Herald*.

I was a Montessori child myself, through the eighth grade, and am both familiar with and appreciative of the program's philosophy. My experiences as a day camp leader and outdoor school counselor have firmed my resolve to enter a career in early childhood education. I believe my background in Montessori as well as my training and experiences in working with children enable me to make a worthwhile contribution to your school.

In addition, as a Native American, I have taken special efforts to learn the history, crafts, songs, and dances of my heritage. By teaching songs, stories, and crafts, I am able to share with others the richness of my native culture. I have had experience directing such activities with children of various ages in my previous position.

I would like to visit the school and talk with you at your convenience. I am available any afternoon and can be reached at 555-7465. Thank you for your consideration; I look forward to meeting you.

Sincerely,

Mary Jo Baptiste

990 Woody Road
Dallas, Texas 75253

15 May 20--

Anita Blakeley
Manager, Blakeley Distributors
886 Denton Road
Dallas, Texas 75259

Dear Ms. Blakeley:

I would like to apply for the position of assistant manager advertised in the May 9 edition of the *Times Herald*.

As indicated in the enclosed resume, I have had some previous managerial experience. At Taco Time, my duties frequently included taking over full responsibility for restaurant operations in the absence of the manager. I became adept at dealing with a variety of crises, from finding substitutes for workers who failed to report to work during rush hour to dealing successfully with surprise inspections from the health and fire departments.

As a recent high school graduate, I may seem young, but I would like to emphasize my commitment to a long-term relationship with Blakeley Distributors. I would like to use my organizational skills, business training, and interpersonal skills to serve your company to the best of my ability.

I hope to have an opportunity to talk with you at your convenience about my experiences and training and how they qualify me for the job. My telephone number is 555-2369, and I am available most mornings.

Thank you for your consideration.

Sincerely,

Brian McGavin

CLAIRE RENARD

618 N.W. Eighth Street, No. 215

Boca Raton, FL 33486

Telephone: (561) 555-1400

ClaireRenard@xxx.com

May 12, 20--

Mr. Harold Washington, Assistant Manager
Florida State Bank
224 N.W. Fifth Street
Boca Raton, FL 33486

Dear Mr. Washington:

I am writing in response to your advertisement for bank tellers that appeared in the *Times* on May 6. My resume and two letters of recommendation are enclosed, as requested.

As indicated in my resume, the focus of my course work has been business and accounting. My experiences as treasurer of the student body and on the school's student finance committee have provided an excellent opportunity for me to exercise the skills learned in the classroom. I was responsible for managing the budget for the entire student body, authorizing disbursements, developing a financial plan for the year, and providing monthly financial reports.

I would like to arrange an interview at your convenience so that I may learn more about your expectations for prospective tellers. I can assure you that I will meet your qualifications. I may be reached at the above number in the afternoons and any time after May 21st.

Thank you for your consideration.

Yours truly,

Claire Renard

Laura Chen

5527 N.W. Oak Creek Road • Ashland, Oregon 97520
(503) 555-9982 • laurachen@xxx.com

May 18, 20--

Mr. Everard Carlisle, Director
Sierra Club International
Central Office 3, 58 Geary
San Francisco, California 94101

Dear Mr. Carlisle:

The position announced in the May 2 *Chronicle* appears to be the perfect opportunity to put my skills in science and business, together with my abiding interest in the environment, to work for the betterment of the earth. I am enclosing my resume in application for the entry-level position in your research and economics division.

As my resume indicates, I have an extensive background in the earth and natural sciences, as well as a strong record in business and economics courses. Capstone economics, in particular, was a challenging course that allowed students the opportunity to unravel economic mysteries by learning and practicing careful economic reasoning in analysis of particular economic situations. I chose as my topic of endeavor to anticipate and evaluate the impact of the balanced budget amendment on federal environmental programs. It was a fascinating project, and I would enjoy having the opportunity to share the findings with you.

I am planning a trip to the Bay Area early next month and would like to visit with you at that time, if possible. The dates of my trip are not yet settled, so I can arrange my schedule to your convenience. Please write to me at the above address, or call me at (503) 555-9982. I look forward to speaking with you.

Sincerely,

Laura Chen

SUZANNE BARSTOW

2248 W. Billtown Road, Apt. 16 • Louisville, KY 40215
(502) 555-7751 • SuzanneBarstow@xxx.com

June 3, 20--

Ms. Theresa Valdez
Staff Nurse
Louisville Care Center
16815 W. MacKay
Louisville, KY 40215

Dear Ms. Valdez:

I would like to submit my resume to you in application for a position as a nurse's aide at the Louisville Care Center. I spoke with your assistant, Jenna Bradley, who indicated that there were two such positions available and that I should write to you directly.

My experiences as a candy striper at Louisville General have made me aware that working in a health care facility is often very tough, both physically and emotionally. I believe, however, that I am equal to the challenge, and I would very much like to make a contribution to the success of Louisville Care Center.

I would like to come in and speak with you about my qualifications and how I can best fulfill your expectations for this position. I look forward to hearing from you. I am available at the above number most mornings. Thank you for your consideration.

Yours truly,

Suzanne Barstow

Toby Waterson

200 South Third Avenue   (213) 555-9226
Arcadia, CA 91006   tobywaterson@xxx.com

❖ ❖ ❖

May 22, 20--

Mr. Bradford Williamson, Personnel Director
Electronics Enterprises
1810 South Olive Street
Los Angeles, CA 90015

Dear Mr. Williamson:

I am writing in reply to your advertisement in the Sunday *Times* for
technicians. Please accept my resume in application for the position.

I have two years of classroom training in Design and Technology,
a program designed to allow students to define and solve their own
technological design problems. I have also had course work in electronics,
engine mechanics, and computer-assisted drafting. Two of the projects
I developed in these courses (a solar-powered car and a computer-
directed light and sound presentation) have been submitted to national
competition.

I would appreciate receiving an opportunity to meet with you and discuss
my qualifications for the position of technician. I may be reached at (213)
555-9226 in the afternoons to arrange a meeting at your convenience.
Thank you for considering my application.

Sincerely yours,

Toby Waterson

3320 Delaware Avenue
Buffalo, NY 14222

May 12, 20--

Ms. Susan Simonson, Manager
Musicland
128 North Seventh Avenue
Buffalo, New York 14225

Dear Ms. Simonson:

In reply to your advertisement in the *Buffalo News* of May 16, I am enclosing my resume to apply for the position of evening salesclerk.

I have had a serious interest in music for many years and have received formal training in both classical and jazz singing. My listening interests in music are much broader, and I keep up to date on contemporary musicians from rap to rock. I believe my knowledge of music would be of great service to your customers.

I would like to set up a time at your convenience to visit the store and talk with you about the position. I am currently working as a singing hostess, but would enjoy the opportunity to work in retail sales for a company involved with music. I can be reached at 555-2193 after 3:30 most afternoons.

Thank you for the opportunity to apply.

Sincerely,

Michelle M. Hibbard

PAUL JEROME

412 Lincoln Road
Las Vegas, NV 87701
(505) 555-6623
pauljerome@xxx.com

May 22, 20--

Mr. Eric Swenson
Personnel Director
The Mirage One
18677 Mirage Court
Las Vegas, NV 87702

Dear Mr. Swenson:

I am writing to apply for a position with one of The Mirage's restaurants. I am interested in serving as a waiter, busboy, or kitchen assistant. John Rivers at Circus Circus suggested I write to you concerning the availability of summer employment.

I worked for Mr. Rivers last summer, and though he was pleased with my work, I would prefer to gain more experience in the restaurant area of hotel operations. I am currently working at Denny's but am eager to return to a hotel environment. I plan to continue my education in hotel and restaurant management.

I would appreciate an opportunity to talk with you about summer employment opportunities at The Mirage. I have long admired the hotel and would enjoy doing my best to serve your restaurant's guests. Please call me at 555-6623 at your convenience.

Thank you for your consideration.

Sincerely,

Paul Jerome

1325 W. Casa del Sol Street
Santa Fe, NM 87538

May 20, 20--

Personnel Director
Bellande Enterprises Inc.
305 E. 102nd
Santa Fe, NM 87536

Personnel Director:

Today, my accounting teacher, Ms. Cheryl Cooper, informed the class about several local job openings in the business field. The secretarial position with your company got my immediate attention. I would like to apply for this opening and have enclosed my resume for your consideration.

I have held two summer secretarial positions, both of which provided me with excellent clerical experience. My tasks included word processing, managing a six-line switchboard, operating a ten-key adding machine, extensive use of word processing and spreadsheet programs, as well as light bookkeeping and data entry. My specialized courses in business operations and accounting have given me the specific skills needed to take on the challenges of a secretarial position. I am very responsible and organized, and I believe I will be an asset to your company.

Thank you for taking the time to review my resume. I would enjoy working for Bellande and would appreciate an opportunity to talk with you at your convenience. I may be reached after 3:00 at 555-5121.

Sincerely,

Maruya Angelino

Shelley Tabor

78 N.E. Towbridge Road • Bridgewater, MA 02324
S.Tabor@xxx.com • (508) 555-8281

May 26, 20--

Ms. Paula Marshall, Director
Little Wonder Day Care
26 W. Fifth Avenue
Bridgewater, MA 02326

Dear Ms. Marshall:

I am writing in response to your advertisement in this week's *Bridge-water Times* for a part-time teaching assistant at Little Wonder Day Care. My resume is enclosed for your consideration.

I have been involved with young children for as long as I can remember. I have four younger siblings, ranging in age from three to fifteen. As the eldest, I was often responsible for watching over them.

For the past five years, I have provided child care for two families, including two summers of full-time care for three children. I always work hard at maintaining a happy, supportive environment, often bringing books and various art or music projects to share with the children. I never rely on television as a substitute for supervision.

I have received formal training in childhood development and education from school courses and experience with the in-school day care center/preschool. The Preschool Practicum, one semester working half-days in the day care center, was an exceptional experience that convinced me to pursue a career in early childhood education.

I would like to come and talk with you further about the position and my qualifications. I am available most mornings at 555-8281. Thank you for considering how I might assist the staff at Little Wonder.

Sincerely,

Shelley Tabor